AF596530

Visions of Truth

Visions of Truth

The Use of Art in the Ministry of Spiritual Direction

MARA LIEF CRABTREE

WIPF & STOCK · Eugene, Oregon

VISIONS OF TRUTH
The Use of Art in the Ministry of Spiritual Direction

Wipf & Stock
An Imprint of Wipf and Stock Publishers
199 W. 8th Ave., Suite 3
Eugene, OR 97401

www.wipfandstock.com

PAPERBACK ISBN: 978-1-62032-660-2
HARDCOVER ISBN: 978-1-4982-8542-1
EBOOK ISBN: 978-1-7252-4805-2

VERSION NUMBER 112823

To my only and eternal love, Tom, who taught me the beauty of life, the beauty of faith, and who modeled to me the love of our Savior, Christ Jesus.

Contents

Illustrations

Preface

As an accompaniment and elective inclusion during my doctoral studies, I completed a three-year master's level program in the study and practical training for spiritual direction at an accredited Christian seminary. Research revealed the fact that no texts concerning the use of art in spiritual direction existed at that time.

Following completion of my doctoral program in Christian spirituality and the additional master's program in spiritual direction, I had the opportunity to practice the ministry of spiritual direction, including the integration of various forms of art in specific contexts of the ministry. I discovered the value of using various forms of art, particularly painting and drawings, but also sculpture, photography, and other artistic forms, to deepen and enrich directees' spiritual formation and overall experience in discernment and insight as related to understanding one's life and faith.

Because life includes intensive experiences that involve the senses used in encountering, exploring, and finding meaning and value in art, the use of artistic forms seemed to me a naturally fitting accompaniment for the ministry of spiritual direction. Why not, in view of all that could be gained by the inclusion of various artistic works in spiritual direction, explore the aspects related to such use, their meaning and value to spiritual directors, directees, and their teachers, trainers, and supervisors? A major concern was to "get the ball rolling" in the process of informing and inspiring those involved in the ministry of spiritual direction, addressing the major information, issues, and concerns related to the use of art in the ministry of spiritual direction.

My own education, training, and experiences in spiritual direction taught me that the world of art has much to contribute, in meaningful ways, to the ministry of spiritual direction. I have practiced and written about spiritual direction within the context of Christian faith. The existence of art forms and the countless works in various genres of art, many considered of classic value, often focused on the artist's representation of one or more aspects of biblical truth. If it is true that a picture is worth a thousand words, then how much more is an encounter with art worth in the process dedicated to living one's faith, in very real ways? How much more than merely viewing a work of art, and learning about it, can art used in the ministry of spiritual direction encourage one's desire to mature in relationship with God and increase one's love for God, and one's love for others, by living in ways that glorify the Lord and bless those whom we encounter in this life? I have learned that the senses of sight, touch, and hearing, those senses so often related to encounters with various forms of art, provide additional ways to increase the value and meaning of spiritual direction. The inclusion of art in spiritual direction sessions is not always necessary, but in view of what the use of art offers in the way of meaning and value as related to spiritual life, art certainly deserves the careful, deeply reflective, and prayerful consideration of its benefits, and all the gifts art can potentially bring to the ministry of spiritual direction.

Mara Lief Crabtree

Introduction

Art, historically and contemporarily, has served as a powerful component to support and encourage spiritual formation, conformation, and transformation in one's life of faith, providing creative and diverse resources for the ministry of spiritual direction. It is the purpose and goal of this work to inform those who are interested in understanding how diverse forms of art may be meaningful and valuable in the ministry of spiritual direction, as understood in the context of Christian faith and tradition.

The book is offered as an invitation for spiritual directors to explore the use of artistic resources for the purpose of enhancing the efficacy and richness of spiritual direction. It is meant to serve as a resource for spiritual directors, their supervisors and directees; for teachers and scholars in the discipline of formative spirituality; and for artists interested in the ministry of spiritual direction. The book is designed not only for the practicing director and supervisor, but as a text for use in colleges, universities, seminaries, and other contexts offering courses or programs of education and training in the art of spiritual direction. It is meant to be used in combination with other appropriate texts, thereby providing an additional, creative option to assist directors' and supervisors' discernment, understanding, spiritual growth, and effectiveness in the practice of spiritual direction.

Although the text provides an introduction to spiritual direction for those who are new to the ministry, the book is not meant as a manual for general training, but as a resource to those interested in learning more about the various uses of art in the ministry of spiritual direction. The book intends to focus on one aspect of the ministry: using art as a resource in furthering and meeting the overall goals of spiritual direction, which are the processes of continuing growth and maturity in one's relationship with God, with self, and with others. The text is not an exhaustive study about the use of art in spiritual direction. The actual experience of using art will yield valuable new information, understanding, and greater discernment essential to directors' continuing use of art in the ministry of spiritual direction. This information purposes to prepare and equip the director in the essentials related to art in spiritual direction. Each director's unique ministry will provide the context for the appropriate and effective use of art.

The content will define and examine the ways applied art forms such as painting and sculpture can be employed to enhance and enrich the ministry of spiritual direction. The work will describe how the ministry of spiritual direction may include art forms in exploring the significance of biblical events, as these events provide insights and lessons for the spiritual lives of directees. The work intends to assist the reader in exploring ways in which one's lived theology may embrace the values and meanings of art through the lenses of sound biblical understanding, theology, history, and one's contemporary life and culture. It intends to encourage directors and supervisors to include the use of art for the purposes of theological reflection and discussing insights related to both intra- and interpersonal relationships and vocations. It is also meant to further both directors' and supervisors' realization of the *kataphatic* (God-revealed) and *apophatic* (the mystery of God) aspects of one's spiritual formation and continuing process of spiritual maturation.

The text discusses how the use of art can encourage a directees' interpretive discernment of personal life events, as well as inspiring growth in faith, worship, prayer, and other disciplines beneficial to one's continuing spiritual journey. It also provides instruction for the reader in ways to practically apply art forms contextually, for individual and group spiritual direction. The work considers the potential ability of various art forms to communicate, each communicating strongly and consistently, with the ability to "speak" through visual, auditory, and kinesthetic media to express spiritual truth relevant to one's life and faith, for individual and group spiritual direction.

Although the book attempts to provide knowledge, guidance, and examples for the spiritual director and supervisor, it is understood that the use of art in spiritual direction, although boundaried by certain principles, is unique for each spiritual director and for their directees engaged in exploring art as a resource. As the director engages in the use of art, he or she will develop an understanding of its meaning and value in the ministry of direction.

Each practice of spiritual direction is unique, depending on the director's particular education, understanding of the Bible, theology, personal abilities, experience, sensitivity to the Holy Spirit, and the particular model or tradition of direction common to each director. Therefore, art, as used appropriately following certain guidelines and principles, will become unique in each practice of spiritual direction.

Spiritual directors are encouraged, as they read the text, to meet with other spiritual directors and/or with their supervisors for the purpose of study, discussion, and practice among themselves in using various art forms in direction, prior to the first actual engagement with the use of art in their ministries. It is never wise to engage in a new ministry practice without the benefit of actual experience. Therefore, this book includes information for directors and their supervisors to provide basic training for practicing the use of art in spiritual direction, prior to its actual use in each director's ministry. It is my prayer that directors will be inspired in their creativity as directors, and in their discernment of the Holy Spirit's leading, to sensitively use various forms of art in the ministry of spiritual direction in ways that align with biblical truth as applied to contemporary Christian life and faith.

Mara Lief Crabtree

PART I

Dimensions and Diversity for the Use of Art in Spiritual Direction

Chapter 1

The Ministry of Spiritual Direction

A Place and Space for Visions of Truth

"Pierce a hole in my darkness that I may see the face of God."

—Oswald Chambers (1874–1917)

THE REDEMPTIVE POWER OF ARTISTIC VISIONS

It was a day filled with expectation as my fellow doctor of ministry students and I entered a Russian Orthodox church in Washington, DC, during our two weeks of resident study at Wesley Theological Seminary. We were respectful and wide-eyed as we quietly met the docent, a gracious man who shared with us that he was related to Russian author Leo Tolstoy. The architectural strength and beauty of the church was evident from its exterior and even more so when one entered the church's worship space. Our smiling guide explained the absence of chairs, stating that it was the community's tradition to stand during worship. We were enthralled by the brilliant frescoes lining the walls of the sanctuary, frescoes picturing the heroes of Russian religious and national history. As with all icons, the figures were not meant to evoke worship of the personages represented in the frescoes. The purpose of the art was to open one's heart, mind, and spirit to the greater reality beyond the visible iconic figures: the beauty, the mystery, the glory, and the power of God.

At one point, our docent, obviously reverent in his approach to guiding our tour through the sanctuary, led us to the back wall of the worship space. Across the entirety of the wide wall was an icon depicting Christ's Passion. Jesus' suffering on the cross was pictured with an artistry that was breathtaking in its spiritual power to convey the reality of the cross. Yet, at the same time, the icon drew one into a reality that was quiet and peace-filled, leading to contemplation of the Lord's love and sacrifice on behalf of those who were lost. As our docent pointed to the Christ figure, pictured in his hours of suffering, he began to tell the story of how this magnificent fresco was created. Our guide explained that a fresco artist, one specifically gifted and trained in the depiction of icons, came to the church and worked steadily for a period of time, painting the background areas of this representation of the Lord's passion. Then the artist began painting the cross and the figure of Jesus Christ. With no explanation and having much additional work to complete on this depiction of the passion, the icon artist left the church, without a word to anyone. He could not be contacted for an explanation. The icon remained incomplete, the passion story awaiting full artistic revelation of the miracle of Christ's sacrifice.

Many months later, our guide recounted, the icon artist returned. He explained that as he began painting the cross and the figure of Christ, he simply could not continue. The artist confessed feelings of guilt and shame. He felt unworthy to create an icon representing the Son of God. He felt convicted that he could not depict Christ's suffering on his behalf for the artist believed he had been acting in ways that brought grief to the Lord's heart. At that time, he was living with a woman outside of marriage and therefore knew he was violating the very meaning, power, and reality of the sacrifice Christ had willingly made for him. The artist believed that under these circumstances, it was not right for him to continue work on the icon. In sadness he fled the church as the convicting power of the Holy Spirit impressed the reality of his disordered life deeply upon his heart.

Buoyed by the grace of God working daily in his life, the artist journeyed through a season of spiritual repentance, facing the ways in which he had failed to live in the reality of Christ's total sacrifice on his behalf. As the prodigal son in the Gospels, the icon painter discovered the mercy of the Father and embraced the reality of the passion: God's loving, abundant redemption from sin freely available through faith in Jesus Christ. With a repentant heart, the artist's passion to complete the fresco was renewed. He was spiritually restored, knowing God had carried him through this journey of shame, then conviction, then repentance, followed by joy. He had been chosen for the privilege of painting the icon and could now openly use the artistic gifts God had given him, but with purity and integrity of heart expressed in his work. The icon of the passion was completed. Here, many years later, my friends and I stood, astounded by how the Holy Spirit had used the icon, even its unfinished depictions, to open an artist's heart, mind, and spirit to truth.

That day, I began to embrace a new understanding of how God could use icons and diverse artistic works, their Spirit-inspired communication mediated by man or woman, in the work of redeeming and transforming human lives. The tour inside the Russian Orthodox Church sanctuary taught me that the Holy Spirit can employ art forms in the unfolding redemptive process of spiritual formation to convict, encourage, comfort, teach, and guide in the process of discerning spiritual reality. The Spirit speaks through visual, tactile, and auditory media in art, satisfying our hunger to see and to hear, not only with physical eyes and hands and ears but with the understanding of our spirits.

This experience opened my understanding to the power of art as a resource in spiritual direction. No sermon was spoken, no human spiritual director was present, no hymns were sung, yet the reality of Christ's Passion, expressed on a frescoed wall, convicted the artist of his own spiritual need. The message of God was mediated though a silent visual representation which nonetheless eloquently proclaimed the message of the cross. Do we limit the ministry of spiritual direction if it is confined to the spoken word? The artist's experience of healing and renewal, which began in an encounter with art, indicates that paintings, sculpture, textiles, music, dance, photography, and other artistic forms are valid avenues through which God mediates truth to those seeking spiritual reality.

The human spirit reaches out to interact with God in multiple ways to experience the whole of life filled with God's reality. Certainly, the presence of art in one's life invites the recipient of artistic experience to embrace those truths the Spirit of God is graciously waiting to share.

A MINISTRY FOR SPIRITUAL GROWTH

It is important to recognize and understand the ministry of spiritual direction as a resource for spiritual development and growth within the entirety of one's Christian life. Spiritual direction has been defined in various ways. Simply stated, the ministry of direction companions another in the process of his or her continuing spiritual formation in Christ, conformation to the revealed will of God, and transformation through the renewal of the mind as one's character matures in expressing both the fruit and the gifts of the Holy Spirit. Direction's goals concern supporting an individual's development and maturation in their experience of relationship with God and in applying biblical truth to all of life. The latter includes learning to participate effectively in community and experiencing growth in ministering to others through the love and shared mission of one's faith community.

Spiritual direction as a discipline provides ways to strengthen and encourage an individual's or group's daily journey of faith in Christ. The ministry of direction can sharpen one's competency to discern the presence and movements of the Holy Spirit, encourage one's maturation in Christian character, and increase one's ability to relate lovingly and with forgiveness toward others. Gordon Smith has defined spiritual direction as having a very clear agenda: "... *directing our attention to the presence of God in our lives*."[1] It is "the ministry of directing our thoughts and the movements of our hearts toward God and the presence of God in our lives."[2]

Additionally, spiritual direction provides guidance in discerning giftings and vocation, as these relate to the whole of one's life. Daniel Burke passionately asserts "... I believe that outside of the Sacraments there is no greater or more important tool available to help us mature in our relationship with God and grow in grace than spiritual direction."[3] Direction is but one aspect of a rich, full, and balanced spirituality. It is most beneficial when one recognizes and participates in the many other practices and disciplines of Christian spirituality including full engagement in and commitment to a faith community, participation in regular worship, personal and group Bible study, partnering with others in the community to fulfill the church's vision in ministry and mission to others, and growth in the quality of relationships with one's immediate family, relatives, neighbors, and

1. Smith, *Spiritual Direction*, 12.
2. Smith, *Spiritual Direction*, 13.
3. Burke and Bartunek, *Navigating the Interior Life*, xvii.

others. Henri Nouwen and other writers dealing with the topic of spiritual formation, assert the importance of spiritual direction as one of several resources and practices needed for the Christian spiritual life:

> The greatest call of a spiritual director is to open the door to the opportunities for spiritual growth and sometimes to provide a glimpse of the great mysterious light behind the curtain of life and of the Lord who is the source of all knowing and the giver of life. To receive spiritual direction is to recognize that God does not solve our problems or answer all our questions but leads us closer to the mystery of our existence where all our questions cease.[4]

One's spiritual development and maturity require commitment to the nurture and fellowship of a faith community, realizing both the joys and challenges in this commitment including the relationships and events that are part of community life. Spiritual direction should not be viewed as compartmentalized or seen as apart from the whole of one's spiritual life but understood as integrated with all aspects of one's spirituality, reflecting the desire for wholeness in one's approach to life and faith. Spiritual direction increases in meaning and value to the individual if one is faithful to a particular Christian community with all its changing facets in the lived theology of life and growth together.

ART AS A COMPANION RESOURCE IN SPIRITUAL DIRECTION

Art is iconic, drawing the viewer beyond itself to other realities, encouraging the beholder to consider how an artistic creation speaks to personal realities. The use of art in spiritual direction sessions can serve as a resource pointing to God and providing a door that when opened, reveals a pathway to discernment and further understanding of one's spiritual existence. Religion and art bear a natural affinity, a resonance with one another, for together they are dialogical, each one informing the other as both reveal and clarify truths about God and life.

> Religion is life and the life that is lived without question and spiritual wrestling is really a dull life indeed. When our minds and religious senses become dull and corrupt, then the glory of God and the blazing intentions of our Lord for our lives are unable to

4. Nouwen et al., *Spiritual Direction*, 13.

> register in our daily existence. That is why religion and art are part of the wide quest for meaning. That is why we need them both.[5]

The use of art may assist in the believer's quest to further mature in both the contemplative and active aspects of Christian spiritual life. The director serves as an encourager, a companion to the believer helping in the search for those truths waiting to be discovered. In the use of art, the director remains the patient listener allowing personal sacred stories to unfold as directees connect visions of truth, as revealed through artistic forms, with their journeys of faith.

The spiritual director must always keep in mind that directees' reactions and responses to art are very personal and should be treated with sensitivity. In using art, a director will need to carefully explain the meaning and value of art in spiritual direction while conveying this information as a gentle invitation, not as a directive. The director always invites rather than urges or manipulates someone to engage with art, for such approaches negate the purity and spirit of openness essential to authentic spiritual direction. The use of art must be practiced with a spirit of meditation and contemplation. To be effective, the process cannot be rushed.

The individual journeys leading to a maturing relationship with Jesus Christ represent diverse pathways. For many, art may serve as a guidepost in their journeys, marking the way to the discovery of certain spiritual realities in their life with God. Gordon Smith points to the focus of spiritual direction: ". . . to direct is to be a companion with a very specific agenda: to help the other direct heart and mind to listen to the one most needed: Christ Jesus. We are like Eli who urged, indeed directed, the young Samuel to be attentive; to recognize the voice and presence of God and respond appropriately."[6] If various forms of art can assist the believer to "direct heart and mind to listen to . . . Christ Jesus," then art becomes important as a resource for the ministry of spiritual direction.[7]

CONCERNS ABOUT THE USE OF IMAGES

In Exodus, the Lord gives the command: "You shall not make for yourself an idol, or any likeness of what is in heaven above or on the earth beneath,

5. Trotter, "What Is Religious Art?" lines 95–98.
6. Smith, *Spiritual Direction*, 11.
7. Smith, *Spiritual Direction*, 11.

or in the water under the earth. You shall not worship them or serve them; for I the Lord your God am a jealous God. . . ."[8] The making of images was forbidden by God, for the creation of such images by the Lord's people would follow the traditions of pagans, who worshiped inanimate, worthless objects made by human hands. The making of such images indicated a fall to the temptation of worshiping those things that were lifeless, that had no value or worth as objects of worship but could only lead to spiritual devastation and destruction by those who created them and used them for worship.

There are Christians who question the use of images that are portrayed in various forms of art. Is the use of such images in spiritual direction a form of idolatry? It is a question that deserves attention, for certain works of art, often those portraying biblical themes, have been and are considered by many as works of great value that have been recognized and used for various purposes throughout the history of the Christian faith. If one's conscience is unsettled and not at peace by the inclusion of art in ecclesial settings, and in spiritual direction, then one should not proceed with the use of various forms of art but follow the dictates of one's conscience.

The primary concern, the question one must answer for oneself is whether the art form used, and the context in which it is used, ultimately serves the purpose of glorifying God and blessing the individual or group using the art with growth in authentic Christian character and behaviors. If a work of art is used to assist an individual to reflect and pray about biblical truth, and the embracing of the truth in one's life, in ways that encourage one's obedience to Christ, then its purpose is not to engender appreciation, reverence, or worship of the art itself but to allow the artistic work to help one focus on the Lord's truth. It is never the art itself that is meant to be the focus of its use in spiritual direction. The use of artwork is meant to always direct one's thoughts, one's desires, one's prayers, and the whole of one's life to God: Father, Son, and Holy Spirit. Its ultimate aim is to deepen one's understanding of God and one's discipleship as a follower of Jesus Christ. To move ever forward in a walk of holiness before God and others defines the reason for the uses and benefits of art in spiritual direction.

8. Exodus 20:4–5 NASB.

THE ROOTS OF SPIRITUAL DIRECTION: A BIBLICAL PERSPECTIVE

In order to understand the ways in which art may be used in the ministry of spiritual direction one must begin from a biblical perspective. Spiritual direction, in Christian context, finds its roots in the Old and New Testament Scriptures. Traditional and classic approaches to spiritual direction can be traced to numerous examples of the guidance provided by God to his people and by those leaders who, in faith, served God's people through an understanding of and obedience to his laws. Although spiritual direction has developed diverse approaches throughout Christian history, and continues to develop new approaches contemporarily, viable Christian spiritual direction looks to the reality of the canon of Scripture for its roots and for testing its authenticity.

Spiritual direction may be defined as a graced process, one that provides guidance and support as a person of maturing faith encounters the realities inherent in one's relationship with God. God has revealed God's self in Jesus Christ, and yet God is also concealed as ultimate mystery. For many, embracing the reality of God's mystery presents a difficult tension in one's spiritual life. Although the believer may be comfortable with God revealed, there is often emotional discomfort in learning to be at peace with the unrevealed God, the mystery of the divine persons of the Holy Trinity. It is necessary to mature in ways that embrace peace, as one becomes submissive to the reality of God's mystery as well as to God's revelation of divine self. Humanness, with its limitations, stumbles in the process of learning to know and understand God, until God is revealed in Jesus Christ. The reality of God is also revealed by the Holy Spirit as one continues to walk in faith. Spiritual direction provides companionship and support as one's heart opens to that revealed and perfect love that "casts out fear."[9] A sensitive spiritual director encourages the seeker to find and remain at peace with the vast mystery of the holy, that perfection, eternal majesty, and wonder which is beyond human ability to fully comprehend and can only be revealed as the Holy Spirit wills. Authentic spiritual direction embraces the reality of the Holy Trinity, present and active in the lives of those who know God.

9. 1 John 4:18: "There is no fear in love but perfect love casts out fear. For fear has to do with punishment, and whoever fears has not been perfected in love" (ESV).

Spiritual direction, in its biblical and historical development and contemporary practice, encompasses a diversity of traditions and approaches. The Scriptures provide the richest source for understanding diversity in the ministry of spiritual direction, its beginnings and development as revealed throughout the biblical text, providing examples of spiritual direction revealed in many ways and contexts. By carefully reading those portions of Scripture revealing individuals engaged in providing or receiving spiritual direction, it is possible to gain insight into the meaning and value of the ministry. From these passages one may compare the biblical examples of spiritual direction with its development throughout history and its diversities in contemporary practice.

When used correctly, art has inherent abilities to deepen one's understanding of Scripture. Along with the necessary and careful exegesis of a particular biblical passage, exploring various artworks relating to the passage provides an additional dimension for individuals to practice a prayerful, reflective approach to increasing one's understanding of the chosen passage. Because the Bible contains events far removed from contemporary times, art has the potential to help individuals understand the spiritual meaning of events in their present life as they relate these events to biblical realities. The use of art in direction assists an individual to reflect upon events far removed from his or her life experience yet which may have significance and meaning for one's present life and for one's future.

Although artistic creations, as defined contemporarily, were not part of the lives of God's people as historically presented in the biblical text, the design of the tabernacle, the temple, and the holy vessels used for various aspects of worship, were elements of religious life and served as outward symbols to encourage the individual's and the community's journeys of faith. These items, individually and collectively, possessed significant meaning as material symbols pointing to the greater reality of God. Each space for worship and each vessel for worship was designed by the Lord, with instructions for their creation given to skilled individuals within the community of God's people who would build or fashion every item with precise adherence to God's commands. Unlike art, as developed throughout history for various purposes, including the expression of ideas, events, hopes, and dreams, these spaces and vessels designed by God and created by skilled craftsmen were designed for people's worship of God as they continued to pursue lives that would evidence faith and obedience to the Lord. Historically and contemporarily, types of art often express religious ideas and sentiments and are present in places and spaces intended for the purpose of Christian gatherings and worship. However, much of art, both historically and contemporarily, is created for decoration or simply for enjoyment. Therefore, the spaces and vessels described in the Bible, although visually aesthetic and artful in the precision and beauty of their designs, were created specifically for the purposes of living one's faith, of worshiping and giving glory to God.

The Old Testament

Before moving forward to a more specific study of the uses of art in spiritual direction, it is important to consider an overview of the ministry of spiritual direction as biblically and historically expressed. It is from this foundation that one may move forward to understand the meaning and value of art: its specific uses in spiritual direction.

The Lord communicated to Adam and Eve in the context of a garden, providing directives concerning the realities of life and including those warnings meant to provide the knowledge needed to avoid actions leading to sin and death. As biblical history progressed, God's own hand, writing commandments on a tablet, would appear to Moses on the heights of Mt. Sinai. The word of the Lord directed his people through the voices and actions of various major and minor prophets: Isaiah, Jeremiah, Ezekiel, Daniel, Joel, Amos, and others. The variety in approaches to spiritual direction modeled by Jesus, and later by Paul and other leaders as they provided guidance to Jesus' followers, emphasize the rich diversity in the ministry of spiritual direction.

The Torah, the five books of Moses, records a compelling description of God's direction in guiding his chosen people. The Lord's creation of the Law provided clear direction in living life to its fullest capacity for love and in service to God, family, community, and others. The Scriptures contain examples of God's interactions with individuals and groups indicating the Lord's ways of guiding and directing his people in many circumstances including times of danger and in seasons of new opportunities.

One powerful example of God's spiritual direction appears in the book of Genesis. In his loving creation of man and woman, God carefully nurtures and directs these new lives in such a way as to provide for their continuing relationship with their creator and with one another for their protection, joy, peace, and vocations of dominion and stewardship over God's earthly creation:

> God blessed them; and God said to them, 'Be fruitful and multiply, and fill the earth, and subdue it; and rule over the fish of the sea and over the birds of the sky and over every living thing that moves on the earth.'[10] The Lord God took the man and put him in the Garden of Eden to cultivate it and tend it. The Lord God commanded the man, saying, 'From any tree of the garden you may freely eat; but you shall not eat from the tree of the knowledge of good and evil, for on the day that you eat from it you will certainly die.'[11]

In the above passages, God's directive is clear, authoritative, and specific, indicating that spiritual direction, in the relationship between God and individuals or groups, reflects God's sovereign authority. Following the fall of Adam and Eve, the Lord's spiritual guidance to them clearly explains their new status and its consequences due to sin. However, the Lord's directive also conveys the first prophetic, redemptive word from God, indicating to the man, the woman, and the serpent, that the Messiah would come to defeat the tempter who was set on destroying the two beings created in God's image: "And I will put enmity between you and the woman, and between your offspring and her offspring; he shall bruise your head and you shall bruise his heel."[12] God then explains the consequences of his creatures' actions.[13] These initial examples of God's directives are important for they indicate the sovereign authority of God's power and how the consequences of sin are met with the hope and assurance of God's mercy and redemptive love. Many artistic works throughout the ages of Christian history have emerged from various artists' visions of the early creation scenes in Genesis. For example, the early Italian Renaissance artist Fra Angelico vividly portrays the reality of the fall in a detail of his painting *The Annunciation*, an altarpiece, created between 1430 to 1445.[14]

10. Gen 1:28 NASB.

11. Gen 2:16–17 NASB.

12. Gen 3:15 ESV.

13. Gen 3: 16–24.

14. *The Annunciation* is in the medium of tempera on panel. Once located in the Church of Gesù in Cortona, Spain, the altarpiece is now housed in the Museo del Prado in Madrid.

Adam and Eve Expelled from Paradise, Fra Angelico

The Old Testament model of spiritual direction often focuses on the prophets as they shared the word of God with individuals and the wider community. The Law itself is a main directive as given by God, the Lord's specific instructions to direct a nation of people in the ways they are instructed to live their faith. God's people were instructed to obey the laws in order to prosper, to glorify God, and to fulfill God's purposes for their lives and for the welfare and sustenance of the nation into the future.

The structures comprising the tabernacle in the wilderness and in the later temple emphasized the importance of God's guidance and direction as expressed through the means of various objects which served as visual symbols. For example, the tabernacle laver, tables of showbread,[15] lampstands, altars of incense, and the ark of the covenant containing the tablet

15. Showbread: *lechem haPānīm* לחם הפנים meaning "bread of the presence."

of the Ten Commandments, the rod of Aaron, and the pot of manna,[16] were visual signs directing the people to spiritual truths essential to faith and life.

Within the ancient Hebrew community, priests, prophets, and kings, either by direct statements, influential examples, or symbolic actions, provided the people with God's direction to protect, guide, and ensure the sustainability of those generations in the lineage of the Messiah. Both the Torah and the entirety of Holy Scripture provide clear examples of spiritual direction in its many diverse contexts. The Psalms and Proverbs emphasize the need to quietly wait upon God and obey his laws. The prophetic books illuminate the relationship of the prophets to God God to the prophets and the prophets' ministries in sharing God's message with the people.

The New Testament

The Gospels portray Jesus as the ultimate spiritual director. The Messiah often met with individuals or with groups, asking questions related to their depth of need. Those questions were often incisive, serving as a spiritual sword to open their consciousness, revealing those sins which blinded them to the realities of God. His questions often evoked thoughts and responses that began the process of people's transformation to new ways of understanding, relating, and acting.

Early in his ministry, Jesus formally directed a congregation by reading the Torah, followed with commentary, in one of the synagogues.[17] Informally, Jesus proclaimed truth and prophetic words to diverse individuals and groups in the course of his daily life. His words often uncovered long-hidden secrets in people's hearts. His ministry expressed a model of direction emphasizing attention to and care for people's present lives on earth as well as concern for their eternal destinies. Jesus' model of direction evidenced care and compassion for every aspect of human life: the spiritual and unseen, and the mundane practicalities of daily existence. His ministries of healing and deliverance were often accompanied by frank and honest assessments of a person's sins, deepest concerns, inner yearnings, emotional struggles, and relationships to God and to others. In his style of direction Jesus frequently listened intently to others and asked them

16. 1 Kgs 8:9 and Hebrews 9:4 appear to give differing accounts of the specific items in the Ark. There is some difference in opinion among scholars as to whether or not certain of the three items were actually kept beside rather than in the Ark.

17. Luke 4:16–21.

questions which revealed his bold and prophetic approach in uncovering and addressing a person's immediate needs for guidance, healing, or deliverance.

His direction was often given gently, in interactive exchange with the person receiving the guidance. Jesus often provided a clear prophetic word to those who were in bondage to sin. In some situations, his direction included silence, or instructions for healing. Jesus' spiritual direction often responded to an individual's specific questions with profound, yet practical theological insights. For example, Jesus' conversation with the Samaritan woman evidenced a brief theological discourse that deepened into his frank unfolding of her life situation. As a spiritual director, Jesus' compelling conversation, revealing prophetic insights into this woman's spiritual realities changed her life, resulting in her evangelistic proclamation: "From that city many of the Samaritans believed in Him because of the word of the woman who testified, 'He told me all the things that I have done.'"[18]

St. Paul's eloquent letters provided yet another form of spiritual direction for members of the nascent church, many who had emerged from pagan belief systems to follow Jesus. Paul's spiritual direction to an individual or a faith community was at times also shared in the context of his physical presence with believers. His apostolic concern and care were revealed in both tender words and corrective admonishment.

In his written communication, Paul presented a model of direction similar to Jesus' ministry. He often spoke with tenderness, while firmly directive in his apostolic ministry of teaching, correcting, and advising various new Christian communities. His missives informed believers concerning common struggles in faith as they sought to follow Christ in challenging times. He provided compassionate guidance, with frank statements concerning his personal struggles during a life of apostolic endeavors as the early church grew in geographical area, membership, and influence. It is evident from Paul's letters that he related personally with God's people, understanding the nature and mission of the church as he identified with believers' life difficulties as well as with their joys. In ministering as a spiritual director, Paul's epistles often addressed an entire faith community, individual leaders, or other individuals within specific communities.

In comparing Paul's ministry to Jesus' spiritual direction, there are commonalities. Both evidence the qualities of compassion and encouragement. At other times, Jesus and Paul used strongly worded directives that

18. John 4:39 NASB.

reveal the true condition of people's minds and hearts. Both models provided needed guidance, leading individuals to repentance and renunciation of sinful ways, encouraging the active faith necessary for those committed to following Jesus as Lord. Jesus and Paul both emphasized the necessity for believers to live in a manner glorifying their Heavenly Father. Paul's model of spiritual direction emphasized the reality of Christ: his person, his purpose, and his teachings.

The book of Acts opens to the reader a fuller dimension and understanding of the Holy Spirit's movements in directing and guiding God's people. Paul's epistles also illuminate the work of the Holy Spirit as director, guiding the ministries of apostles, prophets, evangelists, pastors and teachers, as these ministries are active in forming and maturing the body of Christ.[19] John's revelations, mysterious and otherworldly, direct believers to embrace the hope of future realities: the surety of heaven and the second coming of the Lord Jesus Christ. The remaining epistles witness to spiritual formation in the nascent church, particularly the Holy Spirit's guidance as mediated through various leaders. In those early years of the church's formation, believers discerned the direction of the Spirit during turbulent seasons of challenge, struggle, and the dissemination of the gospel message throughout the known world. The revelation of St. John, in all its power and mystery, points to the spiritual realities yet to come and testifies, through John's visions, to eschatological reality. From the above and numerous other examples, it is evident the biblical record provides testimony to the continuing ministry of spiritual direction. It is this selfsame ministry, guided by the Holy Spirit, that contemporary directors seek to emulate in their ministry of direction.

ARTISTIC VISIONS IN CHRISTIAN HISTORY

The ancient visions of biblically recorded events, those past and the eschatological visions yet to come, have often been translated into various works of art which speak to hearts and minds yearning for God. These artistic works bring the light of knowledge and the nurture of truth to those who desire to live in relationship with God as disciples of Jesus Christ. When one explores the biblical texts, post-biblical history, and the contemporary church for examples of spiritual direction, it is evident the ministry is diverse in its models and expressions and open to contextualization dependent upon

19. Eph 4:11–14.

time, place, faith tradition, ethnicity, culture, forms of training in direction, and other factors.

The monastic movement, beginning in approximately 300 AD, revealed the emerging lives and ministries of the desert *abbas* and *ammas*. Their disciplines of silence, solitude, prayer, and study focused on the passionate intent to experience the reality of their faith in God. Although the early monastics have often been portrayed as isolationists, they did not neglect fellowship with one another, as possible within their contexts of living, and an attitude of humility in remaining open to spiritual direction from one another. Their lives, devoted to prayer and contemplation, allowed them opportunities for an intentional existence in which seeking God became the focus of their lives. In pursuing the Lord, they gained wisdom, and that wisdom was available to share with others who sought the desert believers for the ministry of spiritual guidance.[20]

As the Church Age continued, the development of various models of spiritual direction was evident in the ongoing growth of Christian ministries. In the continuing history of the faith each tradition developed its own methods and processes that may be defined as the ministry of spiritual direction. Becoming a disciple of Jesus Christ, no matter the era, required a new believer to seek the spiritual direction of God's revealed word, the inner leading of the Holy Spirit, and respect for the authority of leadership God had placed within each faith community. Bishops, pastors, priests, and other leaders served as spiritual directors and shepherds to members of their various flocks. Diverse approaches or models of spiritual direction developed. As denominations emerged, and as the church continued its global expansion, the ways in which Christians provided both formal and informal spiritual guidance to their fellow brothers and sisters would continue the further development of unique models for direction. More authoritarian models, for example those related to the Orthodox and Roman Catholic traditions, were complemented by the Celtic Christian model of direction in which the director is known as an *anam cara*, or soul friend. The Celtic approach, in which director and directee are considered equals, is relatively informal as compared with other, more formal models.

Various Pentecostal groups and denominations arising from the early twentieth century Azusa Street Revival believed in the concept of spiritual

20. Keller, David G. R. Oasis of Wisdom, contains wisdom from the adherents of the early monastic period. The stories provide insight into the particulars and style of early monastic spiritual direction.

direction but understood the ministry as conveyed to each believer by the Holy Spirit through preaching, scriptural study, formal classes in Bible, and various expressions of spiritual gifts including prophecy and others. All the above-stated stated disciplines or expressions of spirituality are valid to the ministry of spiritual direction. The classic practice of meeting one-to-one or in a small group setting to encourage growth in one's spiritual life, as facilitated by someone considered qualified by specific study and training in spiritual direction, was not a practice common to early Pentecostal groups. The Roman Catholic, Orthodox, and mainline Protestant traditions have been, for the most part, more conversant with historically traditional practices in the ministry of spiritual direction. This does not indicate that one tradition's approach to spiritual direction is more valid than another's, but simply emphasizes the existence of diversity in the ways spiritual direction has been understood and practiced in Christian contexts.

During the Charismatic Renewal beginning in the mid-twentieth century, which included Roman Catholics, Orthodox, and mainline Protestants, spiritual direction experienced a resurgence in the understanding of its meaning and value by participants of the movement. Writers including Dallas Willard, Richard Foster, and others were among those whose writings exposited a new understanding of spiritual formation, discipleship, and direction, encouraging Christians' participation in spiritual direction.[21] The ministry of spiritual direction began to evidence a new sensitivity to diversity: the importance of understanding and embracing forms of Christian spiritual direction arising from various dimensions of religious culture within the Christian and Jewish traditions.[22] Various colleges, universities, seminaries, and other schools and programs now offer degrees, certificate programs, or additional types of studies in spiritual direction and the training of spiritual directors. This renewed interest has influenced directors and their supervisors, as well as those who teach spiritual direction. The resurgence of interest has resulted in the availability of new books, articles,

21. The following represent a few of the authors whose various writings, in the twentieth and twenty-first centuries, represent important contributions to the spiritual direction community: William A. Barry, Fr. John Bartunek, David Benner, Dan Burke, Marie Theresa Coombs, William J. Connolly, Rose Mary Dougherty, Richard Foster, Margaret Guenther, Liz Hoare, Alan Jones, Thomas Keating, Gerald May, Gary Moon, Thomas Merton, Francis Kelly Nemech, Henri Nouwen, Eugene Peterson, Daniel L. Prechtel, and Dallas Willard.

22. A few of the most important books broadening the understanding of perspectives in spiritual direction are *Beyond the Suffering: Embracing the Legacy of African American Soul Care and Spiritual Direction* by Robert W. Kelleman, and Karole A. Edwards.

and other resources to inform and train the spiritual direction community and to encourage scholarship and creativity in new methods and practices in spiritual direction.

Spiritual Direction in Contemporary Context

The later Quaker model, known as the clearness committee, with its emphasis on the shared ministry of direction among community members and contemporary models of direction which include some aspects of knowledge gained from psychology, point to the continuing emergence of creative approaches to spiritual direction.[23] There are differences of opinion among spiritual directors in the Christian tradition concerning whether certain aspects of psychology are appropriate to a sound biblical theology in the practice of Christian spiritual direction.

Contemporarily, psychology and spiritual direction have joined hands with certain faith traditions and individuals who see the possibility of integrating shared wisdom from the ministry of direction and the practice of therapy as a means to broaden and deepen the possibilities within spiritual direction. The contemporary ministry of Christian-based life coaching also shares certain similarities with spiritual direction, although its ultimate goals are distinct from the latter, focusing on the type of interactions that are geared to develop knowledge and skills toward achieving specific goals that are often aligned with an individual's career field. Discipleship training, pastoral counseling, therapy, life coaching, and spiritual direction, although sharing various commonalities, are each distinct overall in their individual values, meaning, and goals as related to development and growth in one's spiritual life.

THE SPIRITUAL DIRECTOR: EMBRACING DIVERSITY

Spiritual direction is accepted as an important part of spiritual life in Roman Catholic, Orthodox, and Protestant faith traditions, including the Episcopal, Methodist, and Presbyterian denominations and other diverse denominations and groups. There are models of spiritual direction

23. *Spiritual Direction and the Care of Souls* by Gary Moon and David Benner, and *The Way of Spiritual Direction* by Francis Kelly Nemech and Marie Theresa Coombs, are examples of texts that address, in part, the integration of certain aspects of therapy and spiritual direction.

emphasizing a contemplative approach focusing on the disciplines of prayer, silence, and waiting upon God. Other traditions may focus more on verbal communication between the director and the individual seeking direction. Still others include the practice of group spiritual direction. One may argue that diverse models of direction are supportable from the witness of the biblical text.

The use of more traditional as well as contemporary models and approaches to spiritual direction are diverse in view of the global community of practitioners and adherents to Christian spiritual direction. The director brings his or her education and training in spiritual direction as well as personality, spirituality, and life experiences to the ministry's practice. The particular model adopted by a director is also influenced by the individuality of both director and directee. This diversity is necessary and embraces the Holy Spirit's creativity within the ministry. It is important that direction's values and goals remain biblically orthodox yet allow for contextualization within the diversity of Christian faith traditions and groups. Just as the use of art in spiritual direction may be a new concept to many in the direction community, the future may reveal other new, creative ways the Holy Spirit guides and reveals truth to the ministry of spiritual direction. It is important to emphasize that various models and approaches must remain consistent to the principle that spiritual direction, to be authentically Christian in character and practice, must be centered in biblical truth. The incorporation of doctrines or practices from non-Christian religions represents syncretism, an attempt to mix the orthodoxy of biblical truth with beliefs that do not represent biblically-centered faith. Syncretism should be avoided in Christian spiritual direction with the understanding that the ministry's purpose and goal is to encourage spiritual growth and maturity in the context of an individual's faith and life.

Each individual Christian faith tradition's theology influences how the ministry of spiritual direction is understood and practiced. In certain faith traditions spiritual direction has a long-standing history, and in others it is less well known, at least by the term spiritual direction. For example, in many revival and renewal movements, which birthed new groups or denominations, the more classically understood forms of spiritual direction often changed.

One would expect the ministry to be diverse, just as the theology and practices related to Christian spirituality have been diverse throughout history, albeit with commonalities, yet reflecting a variety of ways in which to support the ongoing life process of Christian maturity.

A Humble Ministry

Spiritual direction has been called a humble ministry, for it is often ministered without expectation of financial remuneration and not recognized or well known in every Christian tradition or denomination. In some traditions, the ministry is considered necessary for church leaders including pastors, staff ministers, and others who serve in well-recognized positions within a faith community and/or a denomination, due to the fact that spiritual direction provides a level of accountability to others as well as accountable self-care for the minister. Contemporarily, the ministry of spiritual direction continues its resurgence and renewal with the emergence of new articles, books, and programs of training in spiritual direction. However, spiritual direction's diversities, including biblical, historical, and newly emerging practices, continue to define the ministry.

Spiritual direction, depending upon the director's tradition and training, may be informal in its approach, the director simply providing the wisdom and knowledge of someone who has walked in faith, with accountability, and is able to advise and counsel others in spiritual matters, rather than someone with formal training and experience in the ministry of direction. For others, the ministry is practiced in a more formalized manner which includes specific, structured training at a seminary, or through a recognized program providing accredited degree programs, certificate programs, or other formal credentialing contexts to prepare potential directors for ministry.

Considerations in Choosing a Model

Because numerous models of spiritual formation are evident in the history of the church as well as existing contemporarily, an individual's formational experience, if known by the director, will point to the most helpful approach. For example, persons from a liturgical and sacramental tradition need to have the values and realities of that tradition recognized, honored, and understood in the spiritual direction process. Likewise, Evangelical, Pentecostal, or Charismatic faith communities embrace specific theological understandings and ways of service and mission within each tradition.

Directors must be able to "speak the language" related to each of the above contexts while understanding the lived theology of faith and community in those contexts.

It is important for the spiritual director to focus on the uniqueness of each person directed: his or her personality, faith tradition, life experiences, needs for spiritual growth, perspectives in view of gender, ethnicity, culture, geographical location, age, interests, goals in direction as well as any physical or other life challenges or disabilities. There is no "one type fits all" model or approach in spiritual direction. The ministry fails if the director focuses solely on one model and approaches the ministry as a methodology rather than prayerfully seeking the Holy Spirit's guidance while taking into account the uniqueness of the individual. The above-stated reasons deem it necessary for the director to learn as much as possible about the aforementioned qualities and issues in the beginning sessions of a person's spiritual direction journey. These factors provide valuable and needed information to the director, information that will later facilitate the process of introducing a particular art form or diverse art forms into the process of direction.

Not Only for Believers

Individuals who may self-identify as agnostic or may be considered as "pre-Christian," engaged in the journey to discover truth about God and explore spiritual reality, may benefit greatly from the guidance of an experienced director. These individuals may have no relationship with a faith community and may feel isolated as they struggle to explore and understand their longing to know God. For these seekers, spiritual direction may provide a place of safety and encouragement on one's journey to find the reality of biblical truth leading to authentic relationship with God and with others.

A colleague once shared with me the testimony of her relationship as director for an individual who espoused atheism, yet ironically, also desired to explore the ministry of spiritual direction with a Christian director. This individual possessed little knowledge concerning the realities of living a life of faith in Jesus Christ. My colleague explained to this young woman that as her director she fully embraced a Christian worldview. My colleague trusted the Holy Spirit to guide her as director, in wisely listening, understanding, and responding to an individual who was pre-Christian in her worldview and personal life experience. The seeker was also involved in an intimate relationship with an individual of the same mind and beliefs. My colleague later shared with me, careful to not reveal any information that would specifically identify her client, that over the months of direction, the confessed atheist opened her heart and mind to embrace the reality of God. She began to realize that her present relationship represented an intimacy not beneficial to either partner, and therefore she and her friend made the decision to part ways.

This colleague's testimony taught me that one must avoid hasty assumptions about another's spirituality, their "location" in the continuum of faith or non-faith, and where the Lord's grace, often unknown to them and to others in their lives, may be leading. Spiritual directors must prayerfully consider how to accompany the agnostic or a Christian whose initial faith has wavered, helping to guide, support, and encourage them on their journey to embrace the reality of a life in Christ. In hearing my friend's experience, I learned the important lesson that spiritual direction is not only for believers but may be beneficial to individuals who espouse no identifiable faith yet possess some inner, subconscious sense of authentic spiritual reality existing beyond themselves. Often such inner yearnings, unbeknownst to the person experiencing them, are indicators of an individual's willingness to explore a spirituality that may eventually lead to acknowledging God and moving forward to a living faith. This is possible when the ministry of spiritual direction is expressed by a director who is sensitive to the guidance of the Holy Spirit. Direction for the pre-Christian then becomes evangelistic, catechetical, and formational.

"Through a Glass Darkly": Discerning Spiritual Reality

A spiritual director must never assume that he or she completely understands a directee's perception of Christian spiritual reality. We "see through a glass darkly"[24] in our perception of another's spiritual knowledge. It is only through the guidance and revelation of the Holy Spirit, rather than through experience alone, that one gains insight into another's spiritual reality. It is unwise to assume that spiritual direction is only for the person with strong religious sensibilities and practices. It is also a ministry capable of opening the door to God's reality in Jesus Christ for those who appear far from authentic Christian spirituality.

24. 1 Cor 13:12 KJV.

For those who are pre-faith in their acknowledgment and understanding of God, art provides a valuable resource for the ministry of spiritual direction. Engagement with forms and works of art that appear secular in subject matter and composition may arouse deeply hidden longings for spiritual reality in someone previously unaware of or denying these longings. Art, as a resource for spiritual direction, is multifaceted in its ability to touch a person's intellect, emotions, and physical senses. Interaction with artistic works may awaken deep memories of a belief in God, perhaps known only in fleeting moments of childhood and then, due to family of origin issues such as learning, training, emotional hurts, and traumas, an early vision of truth may appear lost to conscious awareness. In reality, any former awareness of truth remains within one's heart, awaiting the Spirit's awakening. The spiritual director who knows and understands the values of art's use in direction and remains patient in the unfolding process of the ministry, will wait upon the Lord's perfect timing, evidencing compassion and support for the pre-believer in his or her journey of spiritual discovery.

Engaging the Whole Person

An encounter with art is a subjective experience in which the whole person, cognitively, physically, and spiritually, interacts with a work of art and interprets the meaning, value, and possible life application of the truth emerging from engagement with art. Because interaction with art is individually subjective, a person's past, present, and future, their perspectives, beliefs, hopes, dreams, difficulties, and joys, become part of the tapestry of interpreting meaning in any work of art.

Unlike worship, which in many Christian traditions engages all the senses, classic or traditional spiritual direction often deals primarily with verbal interaction. Just as worship is enriched by use of one's physical gifts and capabilities to glorify God, spiritual direction, through the creative use of art, engages additional intellectual and spiritual abilities enabling the process to encourage growth in a deeper way. The use of art allows the directee to gain new perspectives about life and spirituality which may not be possible when the ministry is limited to verbal communication. Rather than merely looking, studying, or reflecting, engagement with art in spiritual direction invites us to *behold* the work of art:

> *Behold* is the marker word throughout the Bible. It signals shifting perspective, the holding together or even the conflating of

radically different points of view. It indicates the moment when the language of belief is silenced by the exaltation of faith as these paradoxical perspectives are brought together and generate, as it were, an explosion of silence and light. This silence holds us in thrall, in complete self-forgetfulness. Our settled accounting of ordinary matters is shattered and falls into nothing as light breaks upon us. Beholding is not confined to monastic cells: it is the well-spring or ordinary life transfigured.[25]

USING ART TO PROVIDE DIMENSION AND DEPTH OF UNDERSTANDING

The use of art in spiritual direction may be described as *visio divina*: "divine seeing." John August Swanson describes this spiritual discipline as "divine reading."[26]

> While *Lectio Divina* is a method of praying with scripture, *Visio Divina* (Latin for "divine seeing") is a method for praying with images or other media. While the Orthodox tradition has long practiced praying with images through icons, the western church, and Protestantism in particular, is less comfortable with this type of prayer. But as a cursory glance through scripture will show, images have been an important part of God's way of communicating. Ezekiel's vision of dry bones, and Peter's dream on the rooftop in Acts 10, are just two instances of how images and prayer are vitally connected.
>
> With our culture becoming more and more visually oriented, an intentional way of praying with images is needed now more than ever. *Visio Divina* invites us to see at a more contemplative pace. It invites us to *see* all there is to see, exploring the entirety of the image. It invites us to see deeply, beyond first and second impressions, below initial ideas, judgments, or understandings. It invites us to be seen, addressed, surprised, and transformed by God who is never limited or tied to any image, but speaks through them.[27]

In the process of *visio divina*, as a companion discipline to *lectio divina*, and as guided by the Holy Spirit, one enters a door opening to a

25. Ross, *Writing the Icon of the Heart*, 10.

26. Swanson, "Praying with Art," lines 1–2.

27. Swanson, "Praying with Art," lines 1–21.

broader and deeper understanding of God and the dimensions of life and faith, in both their present and eternal aspects. Art provides a dimension to spiritual direction that is not possible if direction sessions include only verbal sharing and spoken and silent prayer. Art, used in spiritual direction, has the capacity to encourage the visions, the sounds, and the physical engagement with art that invite an exploration of life and faith that would not otherwise be possible.

It is important for spiritual directors to understand that one does not seek God in the art any more than one seeks holiness through practice of the spiritual disciplines alone. In practicing the spiritual disciplines, one gives one's full attention to God, through whose loving presence one is changed. In the same way, art can serve as a means to give one's focus to God, as a way of surrendering to the Spirit and allowing him to use the creations of artists to draw one to the reality of God's presence and truth.

Art forms serve as resources to encourage reflection and to gain new perspectives, including development of a prayerful life, as an individual is struggling to progress in a maturing relationship with God. Art may awaken a desire to pray as well as presenting new ways to engage in prayer. Art forms may stimulate reflection on the past, including the people and events in one's spiritual journey. Engagement with art may awaken an individual to better understand present realities and the many desires and difficulties in one's spiritual life. Art may stimulate one's recognition of a longing for God, one's anxieties about relationship with God, and one's experience of disappointments with various aspects of spiritual life.

Silence in the Contemplation of Art

Contemplating a work of art emphasizes the importance of silence within the self and in the outward context in which one engages in the reflective process with works of art. Silence encourages the ability to reflect deeply, allowing one's heart, mind, and spirit to be open and to discern the "still, small voice"[28] of the Holy Spirit. One benefit of engagement with art in spiritual direction is practicing the discipline of silence, which provides relief from the often intense levels of inner and outer noise throughout one's waking day; noise that interferes with one's ability to discern the Spirit's voice.

28. "And after the earthquake a fire; but the Lord was not in the fire: and after the fire a still small voice" (1 Kgs 19:12 KJV).

> The choice for silence or noise, for carefulness or carelessness, is ours in every moment. To choose silence as the mind's default in accelerating consumer culture—a culture that sustains itself by dehumanizing people through the unrelenting pressure of clamor, confusion, and commodification—is indeed a subversive act. For the reality is that our lives do hang in the balance, between speech and silence, action and reflection, distraction and attention, extinction and survival. We bear responsibility for maintaining this balance, just as our choices for or against silence can affect the choices of everyone around us. . . .[29]

Evocation of Inner Realties

During the practice of silent reflection, use of art may evoke emotions and motivations of which one was not previously aware. The emergence of emotions and motivations into the light of God's truth encourages healing and further growth in those inward spiritual gifts and graces that influence the development of character and the outward expressions, in love and service, of those gifts and graces. Silent engagement with art brings to the surface of one's consciousness realities, needs, desires, hopes, challenges, and difficulties that previously were inexpressible, even unknown at the conscious level.

Experiencing Art as Shared Humanity

Interaction with art in spiritual direction serves as both a stimulator and encourager of growth in one's spiritual knowledge and experience. When experiencing a work of art, one is connecting with the expressed artistic reality of the artist. This connection may move the beholder of the art from a place of feeling alone and isolated in personal thoughts and perceptions, to a place of new understanding as the work shares the message conveyed through its artistic expression. One challenge of spiritual life and its many dimensions is the perception that one is alone in their particular thoughts, feelings, and actions related to spirituality. The Holy Spirit uses art to break through the wall of isolation, opening the consciousness of the one experiencing the art to a place of truth. As art connects the viewer with the artist,

29. Ross. *Silence: A User's Guide*, vol. 1, 11.

the artist's expression speaks into the life of the viewer, letting them know they are not alone in their lives and spiritual journeys.

The Importance of Aesthetic Values in Spiritual Direction

Art contributes aesthetic ambience to the ministry of spiritual direction. The dimension of theological aesthetics is essential to the continuing maturation process in the life of the believer. Knowing and loving God and others requires an openness to the reality of natural and theological beauty. Spiritual directors should be aware that the aesthetic reality of the holy moves one to celebration, to rejoice in God whose beauty is sublime and limitless, to rejoice in the beauty of salvation, to rejoice in artistic expressions of spiritual realities that glorify God and draw us to worship.

Reflecting on works of art encourages spiritual discernment of God's unsurpassed beauty and the recognition of lesser and earthly forms of beauty as experienced through the physical senses and spiritual discernment. For individuals who may feel their lives are far removed from beauty because they have known hurt, betrayal, abuse, disappointment, grief, trauma, or other negative experiences, art may serve as the door to the reality of authentic beauty. One attribute of art is its ability to "lift" one's spirit, thoughts, hopes, and dreams to a place where experiencing the beautiful is possible. Faith is enhanced by authentic aesthetic reality, as that reality expresses the truth of God. When the authentically beautiful is limited in one's life, due to various factors, art provides a means to restore and enhance aesthetic sensibilities. Interaction with that which is beautiful and true can encourage hope, healing, restoration, and wholeness to the human soul, to the person who has been traumatized by sin, evil, or loss of hope. To acknowledge and embrace the beauty of Christian character, the beauty of God's gifts, the beauty of things seen and unseen, opens one to thankfulness and gratitude in worship as well as an attitude of thanksgiving throughout all of life. A work of art may move one to prayer, to worship, and to ministries of active engagement with and care for others which express self-surrender in loving God and loving humanity.

> . . . in the religious experience and in beauty men feel that they find perfection; hence the attitude of self-surrender and joyousness characterizing both. The abandon of the spectator who decrees that for the moment his life shall be that of the work of art, is matched in the mystical experience by the emotion expressed

> in Dante's line, 'In his will is our peace.' And in both the self-surrender is based on a felt harmony between the individual and the object—the beautiful thing appeals to the senses, its form is adapted to the structure of the mind, its content is such as to win interest and sympathy; the divine is believed to realize and quiet all of our desires. But while in the presence of beauty we feel ourselves at home with the single object, in religion we feel at rest in the universe.[30]

The use of art in spiritual direction has the potential to open doors of new understanding and the clarity inherent in visions of truth, visions reminding the viewer of the eternal glory of God, who is perfect beauty.

30. Parker, "Art in the Service of Religion," lines 96–107.

Chapter 2

Art as a Doorway to Exploration and Discernment in One's Spiritual Journey

"Faith is the divine evidence whereby the spiritual man discerneth God, and the things of God."

—John Wesley (1703–91)

ART AS AN OPEN DOORWAY IN DISCERNING TRUTH

Art, appropriately used, reveals truths, and assists directees to interpret feelings and events in their lives. Art provides an open doorway to enter and to explore the various meanings of what is experienced in life, including one's faith, dreams, visions, and hopes for the future. Artistic forms provide a means to emphasize truth, to help one discern, reflect upon, and contemplate truth as truth relates and appliesto all of life, including one's relationships, and overall spiritual journey.

Art is an expression of God's love for his creation. It is through the mind, thoughts, eyes, hands, and voice of the artist that God creates a work symbolic of some aspect of God's creation that moves art's beholder to praise, glorify, and adore the Creator. Art, when inspired by the Holy Spirit, expresses what is inexpressible in words alone. Artistic vision and expression give dimension and voice to the continual longing of the human creature to the creator. God created humankind in his image and likeness to have dominion over the earth and to forever enjoy a glorious fellowship with the creator.[1] Humankind's original unbroken dominion over the earth, in fellowship with God, became marred by the curse of sin and redeemed by the sacrifice of the Son of God. Through Jesus Christ, humankind's desire and longing to express love for God motivates the artist in expressing the reality of God's wonder and splendor through diverse forms of artistic endeavor. Although that expression is not perfect, it becomes, when inspired by the Spirit, a form of giving worship to God.

Painting and sculpture provide both visual and sometimes kinesthetic "doorways" that when opened and entered, aid directors and directees in accessing the cognitive, affective, and spiritual dimensions of the human person: one's inner truth. The use of visual images, and auditory or physical expressions in artistic forms, may serve to stimulate a directee's perception of God's presence, may reveal evidence of God's guidance, or in general, open new possibilities for embracing and understanding spiritual truth.

Christine Valters Paintner explains the integration of art and spirituality:

> For me, both art and spirituality are truly about tending to the moments of life: listening deeply, holding space, encountering the sacred, and touching eternity. . . . We know we have touched this moment when we are moved by something beyond us yet also rising from deep within. . . . We may not know exactly why or how, but we know we have been touched and transformed, invited into a greater compassion for ourselves and the world.[2]

Artistic resources, used with appropriateness and discernment, act as revealers and sometimes as interpreters of particular truths. A work of art can serve as an "icon" in spiritual direction, leading not only to prayer but to breaking the silence of one's heart through encounter with a visual image or images. Artistic icons may also evoke auditory or kinesthetic experiences that encourage cognitive realization and verbal expressions of truth one could not previously perceive and express in words. Thomas Trotter defines the essence of art as ". . . the process of expressing in concrete form or event human emotions and aspirations, ranging from the simple joys of being to complex philosophical expression. A work of art is a concrete

1. Gen 1:26.

2. Paintner, *Eyes of the Heart*, 4.

thing, an event that helps the participant to bridge his experience with that of the artist or the group or the religious values expressed therein."[3]

Art is of particular meaning and value to the life of the church, for art expresses a form of communication. Amos Wilder assets that "When we say Art we say Image; and when we say Image or Symbol we say Meaning, we say Communication."[4] The understanding and use of symbol, according to Wilder, enjoyed, in the mid-twentieth century, a renewal in ecclesial contexts:

> More significant today than the church's activity in connection with the arts is the deeper motivation which is revolutionizing the church's whole attitude to symbolic expression. Even those churches which we call liturgical, and which have maintained a positive attitude toward the arts, have recognized a new dimension in this area. The historical study of Christian art has quickened, and been quickened by, the new recognition of the importance of the symbolic element in religion and life.[5]

In the twenty-first century, an age of visually perceived technologies, art continues to expand and amplify its influence in the realm of religious faith.

The Bible and Art

The Scriptures are filled with both mystery and revelation, with meaningful images expressed through the symbols of ancient language revealing vivid visions of truth. Countless works of art, both well-known and obscure, focus on subjects portraying scenes, individuals, events, and theological themes derived from Holy Scripture. "The closer we get to the edges of the mystery of things, the less adequate our explanations become."[6] The truths contained in Scripture command expression in word, song, instrumentation, dance, architecture, sculpture, tapestries, vestments, paraments, and the creation of spaces for worship. The Bible is rich with artistic expression: the powerful art of the written word, emerging through individual characters of ancient language, each of which serve as artistic symbols in themselves. The iconography of language provides expressions which allow

3. Trotter, "What Is Religious Art," lines 38–40.
4. Wilder, "Church's New Concern with the Arts," 14.
5. Wilder, "Church's New Concern with the Arts," 12.
6. Trotter, "What Is Religious Art," line 52.

a reader's spiritual vision to see beyond the characters and grasp a fuller and deeper reality of God.

God's gifts of visions and dreams as well as the interpretation of visions and dreams, for the purpose of leading and guiding God's people, are evident throughout the Scriptures. The prophet Joel proclaimed to God's people concerning the power of the Holy Spirit:

> It will come about after this
> That I will pour out My Spirit on all mankind;
> And your sons and daughters will prophesy,
> Your old men will dream dreams,
> Your young men will see visions.
> Even on the male and female servants
> I will pour out My Spirit in those days' (Joel 2: 28–29 NASB).[7]

In Joel's prophetic utterance the Holy Spirit's role in providing God's truth in visual contexts is clearly declared. The prophet announces that the Holy Spirit would provide dreams and visions of God's own truth; a promise available to God's people of faith, regardless of age or gender. During Jesus' ministry on earth, he prophesied to his disciples concerning their personal relationship to the Holy Spirit, whom he indicated would live within them: "But when He, the Spirit of truth, comes, He will guide you into all the truth; for He will not speak on His own initiative, but whatever He hears, He will speak; and He will disclose to you what is to come."[8] In Jesus' statement he refers specifically to the communication of the Holy Spirit. He also teaches that the Spirit will "disclose" those things that are to come. In comparing the Joel and Acts passages with John's recording of Jesus' comments describing the Holy Spirit, it is evident the idea of disclosure will include visions and dreams and their content may be shared with others, through prophetic speech inspired by the Spirit.

The Holy Spirit as Divine Interpreter of Art

Christ within the believer, the incarnational reality of God's Spirit alive and active within people of faith, indicates that discernment of truth is possible as the Spirit guides an individual's interaction with artistic works. "The incarnation means that God is discovered once again and calls out to us

7. This prophecy of Joel is repeated by the apostle Peter in his sermon on the day of Pentecost as recorded in Acts 2: 17–18.

8. John 16:13 NASB.

through our contemplation of and action in God's creative activity in our world. By prayerfully discerning the living Word revealed in Scripture and in the Spirit-inspired artistic witnesses of earth, we hear God speak."[9]

The visual, auditory, and kinesthetic aspects of art are interspersed throughout the entirety of the biblical text. In history, the art of illuminated texts, for example, *The Book of Kells* [10] and the contemporary *St. John's Bible,*[11] intensifies the artistic reality of the Scriptures as visual art. Illuminated texts have a way of increasing one's engagement with the written word, enhancing and stimulating one's attentiveness to and memorization of the Word of God through lines, shapes, colors, spacing of words, and even the open spaces between words; all of these characteristics speak to the artistic vision shared through illuminated texts. Donald Jackson, calligrapher and artistic director of The St. John's Bible, testified that "the continuous process of remaining open and accepting of what may reveal itself through hand and heart on a crafted page is the closest I have ever come to God."[12]

> *The Saint John's Bible* is a work of art and a work of theology. A team of artists coordinated by Donald Jackson in Wales and a team of scholars in Central Minnesota have brought together the ancient techniques of calligraphy and illumination with an ecumenical Christian approach to the Bible rooted in Benedictine spirituality. Back in the 1990s, Donald Jackson observed the monks of Saint John's Abbey processing with their Book of the Gospels for Sunday Mass, and he recognized the importance of 'their book.' To create a Bible that would capture the beauty and tradition of centuries of liturgy and carry it into the future—that is the vision that united a calligrapher in Wales with a group of Benedictine monks in Minnesota.[13]
>
> As people look at the images and read the text, they become interested in the ancient arts of calligraphy and illumination and in the way text and image work together in the illuminated Bible. 'The illuminations are not illustrations,' says Father Michael Patella,

9. Blaine, *Imaging the Word*, 9.

10. *Book of Kells* circa 800 AD, was created by Irish monks, and contains the Latin version of the four Gospels. Now located at Trinity College Library, Dublin, Ireland, it is an example of excellence in the category of illuminated texts.

11. *St. John's Bible*, lines 1–3. "In 1998 St. John's Abbey and University commissioned renowned calligrapher Donald Jackson to produce a hand-written, hand-illuminated Bible". The seven volumes were completed in December 2011.

12. *St. John's Bible*, "The Process," lines 1–2.

13. *St. John's Bible*, lines 1–18.

> chair of the Committee on Illumination and Text (CIT). 'They are spiritual meditations on the text. It is a very Benedictine approach to the Scriptures.' A primary spiritual practice of Benedictine monks is *lectio divina*, a prayerful, reflective reading Scripture. The *St. John's Bible* has opened the door to a practice they are calling *visio divina*, using the illumination to open up . . . Scriptures, letting them speak to us in new ways.[14]

The St. John's Bible, illustration

Mental visions arising from within one's internal, spiritual visions of God's truth indicate engagement with both the narrative and didactic portions of Scripture. Although not written for artistic purposes, the Bible has provided a fountainhead for artistic expression throughout history. For example, the psalms, the hymnal of Holy Scripture, serve as artistic, liturgical visions to those who sing and pray its passages. For example, one may

14. Sink, *Art of The St. John's Bible*, xiv.

read the psalms replete with their rich poetic imagery, and each psalm may evoke thoughts, images, and a particular truth to the person reading or singing the psalm. Many of the greatest works of art contain as subject matter the artists' inspired expressions of biblical themes. These expressions in painting, sculpture, photography, textiles, music, and other artistic forms have been created to give both voice and vision to what is revealed in the pages of Scripture.

One Holy Vision of Truth

The Bible presents one integrated holistic vision: God's salvific message: his love, compassion, and redemption in past, present, and future for humankind. It is the biblical text's Holy Spirit-inspired visions of truth that have stimulated artists to use their giftedness to express individual, often nuanced, understandings and interpretations of God's truth. Some artistic expressions are precise and eloquent, interpreting the words of Scripture in colors, shapes, forms, and human figures, revealing an artist's passion to praise and glorify God by expressing these visions of truth. Those artists who may not have God in mind in their artistic expressions often subconsciously give expression to profound truths relevant to the human condition andits needs.

Messengers of the Spirit

Art is simply another way to communicate the truth of Scripture, its message conveyed in words that become paintings, music, sculpture, photography, or other creative expressions. "I maintain that the arts are modes of communication, rendered or expressed in distinct types of 'languages' which are embedded in time, culture, worldview and traditions of development."[15] It is often possible to comprehend in art what we cannot understand through written words, and words inspire the artistically gifted to translate the truth of words into artistic visions. As inspired by the Holy Spirit, the artist serves as messenger and interpreter of the written word, a proclaimer and prophet, a mediator between God and humankind, in expressing visions of truth that originate from heaven. Words give rise to the process of interpretation through written languages but also through visual or auditory expressions

15. McCullough, *Sense and Spirituality*, xvii.

of artistic forms. Words may be translated to visual icons, symbolic representations pointing to the reality of God beyond them. A single word, for example, the universal cry of praise: "Hallelujah," can inspire countless paintings, sculptures, and works in music, dance, photography, or other arts. Art has the ability to translate the praise and worship of God through the mediated communication of a painting, sculpture, or other works of art, allowing truth to be viewed by the eye, touched by the hands, or heard by the ears, revealing the reality of God through an artist's vision. However, it must be understood that art can only express the reality of biblical truth if the artist knows and understands and expresses the truth with clarity, not adding to or taking from proper and precise exegesis of the reality the artist wishes to accurately convey through the media of art.

ART AND THE BRAIN

The discipline of neuroscience continues to engender significant advances in the field of research dedicated to understanding the brain, its structure and functioning that affect every area of life, including spirituality. Contemporary neuroscience research continues to reveal remarkable information concerning the effects of art on the physical structure of the brain, on cognition, intellectual powers, and emotional and psychological health. This research is of interest to spiritual directors to understand how engagement with forms of art can impact and influence the profound reality of a human life, created in God's image.

The statement "Art is central to our lives and should not be an outlier" truly expresses the understanding of art and the passion for art that is espoused by many, not only those in the community of global artists, but by those who engage with art, in one way or another, on a daily basis.[16] That daily engagement can profoundly affect one's cognition: "'. . . there's a unique way that the brain activates when we view compelling artwork, something philosophers have called the 'aesthetic emotion.'"[17]

> Embodied cognition is 'the sense of drawing you in and making you really feel the quality of the paintings,' [Christopher] Tyler explained. For example, viewers appreciate Botticelli's painting *The Birth of Venus* because it makes them feel as though they are floating in with Venus on the seashell. . . . Mirror neurons, cells in

16. Drevitch, "Why a Love of the Arts Will Help Your Brain Age Better," line 67.

17. Jackson, "How Art Affects the Brain," lines 15–16.

> the brain that respond similarly when observing and performing an action, are responsible for embodied cognition. 'Performing an action requires the information to flow out from the control centers to the limbs . . . But observing the action requires the information to flow inward from the image you're seeing into the control centers. So that bidirectional flow is what's captured in this concept of mirror neurons and it gives the extra vividness to this aesthetics of art appreciation.'[18]

Eric Jensen explains that

> Arts enhance the process of learning the systems they nourish which include integrated sensory, attentional, cognitive, emotional, and motor capacities, are, in fact, the driving forces behind all of their learning. That doesn't mean that one cannot learn without the arts; many have. The arts, however, provide learners with opportunities to simultaneously develop and mature multiple brain systems, none of which are easy to assess because they support processes that yield cumulative results.[19]

Art and Emotional Response

Artistic works have the ability to evoke strong emotional responses in spiritual direction. One theory defines emotion

> as a process in which a special kind of automatic 'affective appraisal' includes characteristic physiological and behavioral changes and is succeeded by . . . 'cognitive monitoring' of the situation. Although there is usually lots of cognitive activity going on in the course of an emotion process, the process itself always occurs prior to reflection. It is because emotions are triggered by an automatic affective appraisal that they are in some important ways immune to assessment as rational or irrational. They are, as Edith Wharton suggests, 'deeper than reason.'[20]

Although art has the ability to evoke strong responses, emotional response is not the goal of using of art in spiritual direction, nor is a purely intellectual response to art a goal in spiritual direction. Ideally, the use of

18. Zambon, "How Engaging with Art Affects the Human Brain," lines 33–36, 42–45, 49–52.

19. Jensen, *Arts With the Brain in Mind*, 2.

20. Robinson, *Deeper Than Reason*, 3.

art will result in a profound experience of discernment, of knowledge that links the reality of sound biblical understanding and knowledge to the directee's own life, ultimately resulting in spiritual growth in one's relationship with Jesus Christ. When a directee does experience a strong emotional response to engagement with an artistic work, a wise director will assist that individual in moving beyond a purely emotional response, or a purely intellectual response, to a place of wisdom that helps the individual better understand biblical meanings that are connected to the work of art. Effective spiritual direction using art will assist an individual to discern how a particular biblical passage relates to the directee's own life, including relationships as well as engagement in mission and ministry for the purposes of fulfilling one's vocation for the Lord as well as blessing the lives of others. Ideally, it is hoped the use of art will result in an integrative process uniting emotional and intellectual responses with a profound spiritual discernment of God's love and purposes for the directee's life and ministry.

Integrating Intellectual and Affective Responses to Spirituality

There are individuals who prefer a more cognitive, intellectual approach to life and spirituality. Others may prefer a more affective approach. Unless the intellectual and the affective aspects of one's being become integrated, then, to one extent or another, spiritual growth is impeded. Works of art that evoke a strong emotional response facilitate an individual's reflective process in understanding the meaning of that response relative to his or her relationships and spirituality. An emotional response to a work of art may indicate a need for healing and restoration in one or more areas of life. The use of art, when guided by the Holy Spirit, assists an individual in integrating both intellectual and affective responses to spiritual direction. The use of artistic works is valuable in helping individuals understand their spirituality, including the yearnings, joys, questions, and anxieties concerning their relationship with God.

CHRIST EXPRESSED THROUGH ART'S MEDIATED COMMUNICATION

In Jesus Christ, "the Word became flesh,"[21] truth became incarnate; God the Son appeared and lived on earth in human form. As perfect God, he embodied the reality of the second person of the Holy Trinity: one who could be seen, heard, touched, and beheld in his own suffering as he completed the work that made salvation possible for humankind. This embodiment, the appearance on earth of the Son of God in human form, did not lessen the power of God but simply provided embodiment to God's reality, allowing individuals to see, experience, and understand God's presence among them.

This embodiment of God in human form, the incarnate Christ, who came teaching, healing, and delivering people from sin and evil, continues to be symbolically represented through diverse forms of art. The reality of God's presence and truth may be conveyed through the mediated communication of various artistic forms and works. God is not limited in the ways he reveals truth or ministers his grace, healing, and deliverance. It is possible to understand and receive particular truths about God as mediated through an art form, just as truth may also be received through preaching or teaching in words. The visual gifts and powers God has given to humankind, the abilities to see, touch and to hear, provide doorways for God's truth to be expressed through artistic forms. These forms express truth, sometimes through silence, sometimes as revealed in words or through visual expression, to those longing to know and understand the love and presence of God, who lives to share his life and truth with humankind.

Physicality and Spirituality

Physicality is vitally important to spirituality, which requires embodiment or incarnationality. Christ, the second person of the Holy Trinity, came to earth embodied as incarnate God, the Son. Incarnationally, the reality of God, the presence of the indwelling Holy Spirit, lives within believers to empower the followers of Jesus, making possible a life in which one's thoughts and actions may be expressed in loving ways that minister truth, healing, and the salvific message of redemption to others. An art form is the

21. "And the Word became flesh, and dwelt among us, and we saw His glory, glory as of the only begotten from the Father, full of grace and truth" (John 1:14 NASB).

outward, concrete expression or embodiment, in media, of an artist's vision of truth. Through the mediated communication of a painting, sculpture, tapestry, photograph, or other artistic work, the artist expresses a personal understanding of truth, a worldview and commentary concerning various aspects of life. For the artist whose motivation is to glorify God, the art embodies, on canvas, on paper, in marble, or bronze, in cloth or through musical instruments or dance, the artist's understanding, often emerging from the artist's own experience of God and God's relationship with humankind. As one experiences a work of art, guided by the Holy Spirit, an artistic expression becomes a vision of truth, a means for a believer's growth in understanding God, self, others, and life.

The Importance of Learning Styles in Using Art

In terms of learning styles, individuals may prefer visual, auditory, or kinesthetic models, or a combination of two or all three styles, with an emphasis on one type. Visual, auditory, and kinesthetic avenues of interacting with art forms provide stimulation, both cognitively and emotionally, as one's spiritual growth continues. Interacting with art forms through the avenues of sight, hearing, touch, and movement often evokes deeply repressed feelings and memories, including emotions of humor and joy, reverence and devotion to God, surprise and wonder, gratitude, love, hope, and the promise of new beginnings.

Art as Iconography

The whole of art, in all its forms, when used in the ministry of spiritual direction, is meant to be iconic. However, one does not seek God in the art, any more than one pursues holiness merely through practice of the spiritual disciplines. Art serves as a means to bring one's focus to God, as a way of surrendering to the Holy Spirit and allowing him to use the creations of artists to draw one's attention to God. Art is never the message or the truth itself but, as in the Orthodox tradition of icons, art is meant to draw the viewer's attention to the one who is ultimate truth revealed by the Father to humankind through Jesus Christ and made known to minds, hearts, and spirits by the revelation of the Holy Spirit.

Authentic Visions of Truth

Direction, with or without the use of art, is grounded by the understanding that God is preeminent in the process. The art itself is never meant to serve as the center of engagement but as a symbol the Holy Spirit may use to uncover, to guide, and to inspire a believer to authentic visions of truth. Those authentic visions always embrace engagement with the Holy Trinity; learning to love and serve God, and in him, learning to love and serve others. Keeping these principles in mind will help both director and client to avoid the error of allowing any work of art to become the focus of direction. The quest to understand God's character, presence, and movements in one's life should remain foremost in the ministry of direction.

Questions Arising From Authentic Visions

Keeping in mind that nurturing one's relationship with God is the purpose and the center of spiritual direction, there are primary questions, each one related to the others, that should accompany engagement with any form of art used in spiritual direction: What is the art revealing to you about yourself and your life in relationship to God? Is your understanding of God, life, faith, relationships, etc., developing and changing as you reflect on the art? What affect does your engagement with the art have on your desire for or movement toward a more authentic relationship with God? Additional questions may be considered as part of the reflective process during an engagement with art.[22]

ART SPEAKS TO THE HUMAN CONDITION

Throughout life persons encounter art, usually in a variety of forms. Whether one is consciously aware of and involved with various artistic works in formal contexts, or one's encounter with art is considered more of a mundane experience encountered in daily life with little thought or engagement, art speaks to the human condition generally and to each person individually in diverse ways. Many children, during their early years, participate in experiencing art, either by engagement with works by others, or though self-creating various types of art. Individuals, who at a young

22. A more comprehensive list of questions relating to the use of art in spiritual direction is contained in chapter six.

age show promise as artists, may have the opportunity for special teaching, training, and tutoring to develop their artistic abilities. Those individuals who are not personally engaged in creating works of art can nonetheless interact with many forms of art and by doing so enrich their life experiences, knowledge, and spirituality.

Who has not viewed a painting, studied a sculpture, reflected on a photograph, listened to various genres of music, or admired an architectural work and not been moved emotionally and spiritually by the message of the artist? Art speaks with its symbolic reality to individuals and groups revealing something personal and powerful about life or serving to interpret what one has experienced during numerous events in life. Because art is experienced and interpreted in various ways, depending on one's culture, age, gender, phase of life, and other factors, the messages of art speak in ways that impact one's life and influence one's personal choices. For example, perhaps Leonardo da Vinci's painting *The Last Supper* may inspire an individual to a deeper appreciation of the Eucharist, or hearing Johann Sebastian Bach's *Ascension Cantata* may inspire an individual to greater praise of God and devotion to Christ. Even the humblest and most mundane types of art have an impact on one's daily life and express certain realties about a particular culture, its nature and values.

The Last Supper, Leonardo da Vinci

Worship Through the Creative Venue of Art

The deep longing to worship God in every way possible often emerges through the gift of artistic expression. For those existing outside of authentic relationship with God, there remains a brokenness and inability to understand that longings for artistic expression are one of God's gifts to humankind, enabling praise and adoration through the visions of truth expressed in diverse forms of artistic endeavor. When one expresses love, praise, and thanksgiving to God through the creative venue of art, and if the expression is infused with the anointing of the Holy Spirit, then a work of art speaks truth about God: the reality of God, and his eternal presence throughout the universe. One's inner compass points always to spiritual north: the need and the desire to glorify God that intensely motivates the expression and enjoyment of art. This longing and desire to worship and glorify God is part of humankind's spiritual DNA and as such is essential to the spirituality of those in relationship with God. For the artist, glorifying God is an act of obedience to one's Creator, Savior, and indwelling Holy Spirit.

A Spiritual Resonance with Works of Art

Most people encounter artistic expressions, often a variety of types of art, during their lifetimes. Many individuals are involved in the creation of artistic works, perhaps in various media. It is the Creator's gift of creativity that allows one to long for artistic expression, to appreciate the artistic creations of others, and to express one's own God-given gifts in many forms of art. *The Nativity of Mary* by Andrea di Bonaiuto, and other masterpieces, are not merely artistic, creative works, glorifying God and proclaiming truth through the venues of paint and brush, and with musical notes and sounding instruments. When one possesses spiritual sensibility and the indwelling Holy Spirit,
and engages with works specifically created for the glory of God, there emerges an answering response of some kind from the viewer or listener of the artistic work. There is a resonance, spiritually, with works of art that visually, tactually, and musically speak of the wonder and glory of God. Even those works of art not created by a motivation to glorify God can be used by the Holy Spirit to touch the innermost parts of one's mind, heart, and spirit, often resulting in a healing process for one's soul based on the

Spirit's revelation of truth. God uses those things which may appear, at first thought, to be without redeeming qualities, to help individuals recognize their hidden thoughts and feelings. The Spirit brings these hidden truths to the light of God's reality, where healing, through Christ, can take place.

The Nativity of Mary, Andrea di Bonaiuto

Visual Symbols as Revealers of Truth

Aristotle maintained that "the aim of art is to represent not the outward appearance of things, but their inward significance."[23] During the three-year period I was enrolled in a seminary program to study the ministry of spiritual direction, participation in a group exercise proved to me the power of even simple artistic forms to open one's mind and heart to the realities of God's truth in one's life. At the time I was engaged in a discernment process to determine if God had called me to vocation as an oblate within a specific religious order. This question was of serious importance to me, one requiring much prayer, reflection, and discernment. I was thankful for the opportunity to share this need within a group setting during one of the three yearly required summer sessions in the spiritual direction program. Each member of the group was afforded the opportunity to allow another group member to serve as their spiritual director. I shared with fellow students my particular spiritual need for discernment: Was God calling me

23. Goodman, "7 Ways Art Supports Interdisciplinary Work," lines 4–5.

to a particular religious order, the focus of which was the vocation of contemplative prayer? As a fellow student and I shared our thoughts concerning my need for discernment, at one point he referred to a portion of the printed pattern on the outfit I was wearing. The outfit consisted of a shirt and a long circular skirt. The material of both garments were printed with various nautical symbols. One of the symbols represented was a sextant, a nautical instrument used to measure the angles between two visible objects. By using a sextant in finding an angle and considering the time when the measurement was made, one can determine what is called a position line on a nautical chart. Serving as spiritual director, my fellow student asked me the question, "One of the symbols on your sleeve is a sextant which measures degrees of angles. When you prayerfully reflect on whether you have a call to vocation as an oblate in this religious order, to what degree do you feel pulled in making a decision to join the order?" It was a stunning question that cut to the very heart of my discernment issue. I had never before considered the problem in quite the way my group member phrased it, as he used a very simple piece of artwork, printed on clothing material, to raise the question that urged me to think deeply about how strongly I felt drawn to affiliation with the order. I thought for a moment, looking at one of the printed sextant patterns on my skirt, and replied, "about 60 degrees," indicating the strength of my inner sense of spiritual "pull" toward joining the order. To me, this revelation clarified my position inwardly and indicated the degree of strength in my motivation and spiritual passion toward the oblate vocation.

This particular experience is remembered, now many years later, in vivid detail because its revelation was so powerful in providing guidance. As one drawn to and having a preference for visual revelation, my fellow spiritual director could not have asked a more relevant question. The question focused on an inner longing to know my "spiritual position," and to determine the "degree" of my assurance in taking a step that represented a discerned call of God, resonating with my inner desire to do so. The experience also taught me that spiritual directors may use mundane objects of art, as well as classic works of art, in the process of helping directees gain insight, discernment, and forward movement when the need arises, to make important decisions. In this case, I was wearing the very art form that, when used sensitively by my director under the guidance of the Holy Spirit, provided a question which empowered me in the discernment process. The Spirit-led creativity of this student director, in using a common, personal object of everyday art, amazed me in both its simplicity and profundity and its ability to provide a most needed vision of truth for my journey of decision.

Artwork, when used in a manner that honors the Holy Spirit's ability to inform, teach, and guide, has the potential to produce similar results in all forms of spiritual direction. The power of the visual, as a gift from God, initially reveals to the eyes what is interpreted by the brain and further revealed by the Holy Spirit, leading to discernment of truth in both one's heart and one's spirit. The goal of appropriate use of art in spiritual direction assists individuals to know and follow the revealed pathways of God in their lives.

Engaging with Art Involves the Whole Person

Psychologically, spiritually, and emotionally reflecting upon and contemplating truth is not merely a cognitive process but involves all the senses, including knowledge gained from interaction in relationships and other important events one has experienced. Receiving and understanding truth is a much more intense and complicated process than mere mental assent to a certain fact or belief. Reception of truth and then the process of acting on truth in one's life also require faith: "People recognize that a picture is an icon, but they don't know what it means so they just switch it off."[24] The acceptance of truth, when the subject of that truth cannot be visibly seen, requires the motivation and actions of faith. Rather than mental assent, faith requires moral actions. As one acts upon faith it is often the senses that reveal the reality of that faith. For example, one may pray for a particular event of healing. In God's action of answering the prayer, the physical evidence, as assessed by the senses, reveals further the reality of what one first believed: that God answers specific prayers. It is in the things hoped for, in the spiritual evidence of those things we do not see but know that exist or will exist, that we find faith to continue our struggle to learn and to grow in Christ.[25] It is often artwork, simple or profound, urging us forward to greater expressions of faith in God.

24. Martin, *Sacred Doorways*, xv.

25. "Now faith is the substance of things hoped for, the evidence of things not seen" (Heb 11:1 KJV).

Relating Art to Personal Needs

Engagement with art may be used in spiritual direction to clarify a particular aspect of life and faith. For example, a young mother, desiring to attain spiritual growth as a parent, may discern, through engagement with a painting of the Virgin Mary and the infant Jesus, the reality of maternal love. Further reflection and contemplation of that work of art, as accompanied by prayer, provides her with an opportunity to deepen her faith in the reality of maternal love. The art may stimulate a process resulting in her understanding of maternal love as a gift from God, present and available to her.

A friend once explained to me how important an icon of the Virgin Mary had become to her spirituality and healing. She and her mother experienced tumultuous emotions as they struggled in their relationship. My friend shared that she felt the absence of a mother's love and yearned to experience and understand authentic maternal love. When she gave birth to her own daughter, this quest to understand maternal love intensified. Years later, when her daughter reached adulthood, she discovered the icon. In contemplating the iconic representation of Mary's face, her features and demeanor, expressing the relationship between mother and child, the Holy Spirit revealed the authentic tenderness, unconditional acceptance, and faithfulness present in a mother's love. Through this encounter with iconic art, she matured in her understanding of maternal love, asking her daughter's forgiveness for her faults and errors in their relationship.

Awakening Spirituality

One's spirituality may be awakened in a variety of ways: through visual means, through cognitive and intellectual means, or through kinesthetic experiences, all of which may be part of one's journey of engagement with art. This is why dialogue, discussion, and reflection, including silent and spoken prayer, may be greatly enhanced and lead to a clearer revelation of God and spiritual life, if spiritual direction includes the resource of art. Spiritual direction is diverse and multifaceted; the director cannot make assumptions or approach the ministry with legalistic and judgmental attitudes concerning a directee's current experience or place in the journey toward knowing, loving, and serving God. This is why the opportunities available through various art forms have the potential to contribute significantly to an individual's journey of faith. The use of art can prevent directors from tendencies to assess a person's spirituality before knowing or understanding that person's faith tradition or their desire to move toward embracing a life of faith. Art that appears secular in its subject matter may have the potential to awaken deep longings for God within an individual's mind and heart. If a picture is worth a thousand words, then it may also be worth a thousand thoughts. Sometimes the desire for God has become so deeply embedded within a person's unconscious knowing, covered over by layers of defenses due to various events in life, that merely trying to discuss these longings towards God are not possible as an individual participates in spiritual direction. Art, in painting, sculpture, textiles, photography, music, and other forms, has the ability, through the Holy Spirit, to uncover and awaken those deep longings, revealing truth in ways not possible in conversation alone.

A Doorway to Discover Meaning

Art can reveal truths and help interpret feelings and events by serving as a doorway in which to explore fields of meaning, the many diverse meanings related to waking experiences in life as well as to dreams, visions, and hopes for the future. Art may whisper or speak boldly to sight, to hearing, and to touch, sometimes moving one to the silence of reflection. In these and other ways, art provides avenues for connecting with truth that may not be easily accessed through the usual methods in spiritual direction. Art may serve as a motivation to deeper engagement with prayer. A work of art in and of itself may express prayerfulness, praise, thanksgiving, longing for the holy, or other needs and emotions. Encounters with art invade one's thoughts and emotions, often with ideas leading to meditation, intercession, or simply silent contemplation. Contemplation, although it may be experienced in the context of engagement with art in spiritual direction, is considered by Thomas Merton, to ultimately transcend art.

> Contemplation is the highest expression of man's intellectual and spiritual life. It is that life itself, fully awake, fully active, fully aware that it is alive. It is spiritual wonder. It is spontaneous or at the sacredness of life, of being. It is gratitude for life, for awareness and for being. It is a vivid realization of the fact that life and being in us proceed from an invisible, transcendent and fully abundant Source. Contemplation is, above all, awareness of the reality of

> that Source. It knows the Source, obscurely, inexplicably but with a certitude that goes beyond reason and beyond simple faith. For contemplation is a kind of spiritual vision to which both reason and faith aspire, by their very nature, because without it they must always remain incomplete. Yet contemplation is not vision because it sees 'without seeing' and knows 'without knowing.' It is a more profound depth of faith, a knowledge too deep to be grasped in images, in words or even in clear concepts. In other words, then, contemplation reaches out to the knowledge and even to the experience of the transcendent and inexpressible God.[26]

LIMITATIONS AND CAUTIONS IN THE USE OF ART

It is important to remember that the use of art in spiritual direction ". . . is not about suspending critique, [of the art] but about exercising it as it issues from a silent space of love, a reality yet unseen (Heb. 11:1) . . ."[27] The goal of all interaction, reflection, meditation, and contemplation related to the use of creative works in spiritual direction is for art to serve as one pathway to discover God and to stimulate growth in one's relationship with God. Art can assist the seeker in acquiring knowledge about Jesus Christ, and in motivating one's faith to believe God's promise of blessings for the purpose of experiencing both a present and future lived in his presence.

Maintaining Focus in Spiritual Direction

A serious caution is called for by both spiritual directors and their clients who choose to use a single art form or various art forms in the ministry of spiritual direction: one must constantly keep in mind that art, in itself, is not to be the primary focus in the process of direction. It is understood that the primary resource upon which spiritual direction must focus is the canon of Holy Scripture. However, artistic resources, when properly related to biblical truth and used with appropriateness and discernment, act as revealers and sometimes as interpreters of the biblical text and its meanings.

In any endeavor involving spirituality or religion, it is possible that meaningful symbols or certain practices, although essential and needful to a life of faith, may become an individual's central focus rather than realizing

26. Merton, *New Seeds of Contemplation*, 1–2.

27. Ross, *Writing the Icon of the Heart*, 9.

that symbols and practices are merely ways to maintain one's focus upon God. It is the love and presence of God, the spiritual reality of divinity, not merely the practices, ceremonies, or symbols of religion, that comprise the central meaning of spiritual direction. Maintaining a God-focused approach to direction, based on biblical truth, results in opportunities for spiritual growth. A God-focused approach results in development of a more intimate relationship with the Lord, a maturing understanding of God's character and ways, and increased sensitivity to the voice and guidance of the Holy Spirit. Growth and maturity in knowing and loving God as one's supreme focus in life is the reason for the ministry of spiritual direction in the Christian tradition. Art, in and of itself, is not the source from which truth is derived, nor the foundation of wisdom from which visions of truth become apparent. Spiritual direction, to remain orthodox and relevant to the Christian faith, must take its foundation from the biblical texts. Sound direction will test every use of art, every form of direction, and every experience in direction, by comparing it to the Scriptures: whether or not any and all of these uses and forms are faithful to the truth revealed by the Holy Spirit in the Word of God.

Awareness of Theological Meaning in Art

When choosing a particular work of art it is the spiritual director's responsibility to research the example to determine any information available about the artist's intended meaning within the work. Knowing the background of the artist, information about the artist's beliefs and intentions to portray certain theological themes, provide the preparatory work necessary to introduce an artistic work within the ministry of spiritual direction. Those ideas, opinions, and beliefs the artist supports may be counter to the ideas, opinions, and beliefs held by the individual engaging with the artwork. Such differences do not indicate a particular artwork cannot be valuable to the process of spiritual direction, but knowing the artist's intent is essential in assisting the directee to have a clear understanding of the artwork. A directee may not accept the theological intent of the work if the artist's intent is known, and yet may find value and meaning in the work, beyond the artist's intent, that may be applied to one's life and faith. An important key in the use of art is remaining cautious about subjectivity as the directee engages with the art. Beyond the artist's intended objective meaning for the work, it is understood that the directee's response to engagement with the work will include personal, subjective interpretations that relate to the individual's life and spirituality. It is essential, when a directee considers the meaning of art in a subjective way, to compare his or her interpretation, especially theological interpretations, with biblical realities that relate to the themes, ideas, and any assumed realities the directee believes are conveyed by the art. The spiritual director must consider the objective reality of Scripture as compared with the subjective interpreted meaning as conveyed by the artist or by the directee. In this process, the director has the responsibility to allow the directee to fully and freely explore the implications of an artwork, being careful to offer guidance if the directee's subjectivity in interpretation moves away from objective biblical truth. A work of art may interpret a biblical theme subjectively, rather than the art aligning with the biblical, theological, and historical realities of the subject or subjects represented. Artists are influenced by their worldviews, by the era in which they live or lived, by their culture, as well as by their personal spiritual and psychological realities. These factors impact the message conveyed by the work of art. For example, Ann Brown discusses Lucas Cranach the Elder's (1472–1553) *Das Paradies*, housed in the Kinsthistorisches Museum, Venice, Italy:

> This detailed picture tells the story of the first three chapters of Genesis. It is rich in religious symbolism: the neighing horse symbolizes lust, the partridge deceit, peacocks pride and bears evil, while the unicorn and stags stand for lost purity and piety. The goat behind the fallen Adam and Eve shows that they are sinners under God's judgment. God is depicted as an old man, and Satan as a golden-haired maiden, a mirror image of Eve.[28]

28. Brown, *Apology to Women*, 11.

Das Paradies represents a highly symbolic interpretation of the Genesis passages. The symbols of the horse, the partridge, peacocks, bears, unicorn, stags, and goats are not mentioned in chapters 1–3 of Genesis. The depiction of God, who in reality is Spirit, is anthropomorphic while Satan appears not as a servant but as a woman. In the use of this work of art and similar highly symbolic works, comparison with biblical realities, especially the particular chapters or passages related to an artist's work, will provide the needed guidance to avoid a subjectivity that misrepresents the true meaning of the biblical text. While the themes of lust, pride, evil, lost purity and piety, sin and judgments, are valid themes present in Genesis, a spiritual director and directee must be cautious to separate what is validly presented in the biblical text from an artist's symbolic interpretation of theological ideas, themes, and realities.

PART II

Eternal Images–Present Visions

Chapter 3

Art and Spiritual Direction

Visions in Scripture, History, and Contemporary Life

"*. . . when you gaze at Jesus your Saviour stretched out like a sheet of parchment on the Cross, inscribed with wounds, illustrated in His own loving blood. Where else, I ask you . . . is there a comparable book of love to read from?*"

—Jordan of Saxony (d. 1237)

A BOOK OF VISIONS

Biblical visual images are powerful and often mysterious: chariots of fire, clouds of witnesses, angelic beings with flaming swords, mysterious otherworldly images that often seem beyond precise interpretation and understanding, as do many of the images in the Revelation of St. John the Divine and other biblical passages. These images stimulate the spiritual imagination and introduce a reality that is numinous, otherworldly, and far from earthly, mundane experiences. They point to a reality that exists beyond one's common daily experience, perhaps in one's dreams and visions of past or future, or the visions emerging from one's prayer life in the present. These biblical visions, painted in words, may lift one's thoughts to a world that truly exists but is discerned in the depths of one's faith, rather than physically present.

The Old Testament prophets were often called "seers," visionaries who sought and proclaimed God's truth. Artistic works sometimes serve to reveal a form of prophetic reality, providing a context for clarity in seeking that which is real and true. Historically, artistic forms have often served as visual revealers and reminders of spiritual truth. Art forms may be implemented to explore the meaning and value of what is both thought and seen, heard and touched, as well as the meaningfulness of vision: the reality that is often perceived inwardly, and points to spiritual truth. As a visual or physically expressive representation of truth, art may provide a pathway to the exploration of spiritual truth, both in individual lives and in faith communities.

These spiritually discerned images are often the subject of art in history. When an artist interprets these images through his or her own artistic vision, they encourage the viewer to contemplate the artist's interpretation of the biblical vision. These images and their interpretation also assist the viewer to carefully reflect on the possible meanings inherent in the work of art as the art is related to the viewer's spirituality. It is necessary to carefully interpret the meaning of these images for the purpose of understanding their biblically contextual implications. These same images may also evoke very personal, experiential meanings relevant to an individual's life and faith.

Reading the Bible encourages engagement with visual images relating to the context of each passage read. The text presents stunning descriptions of events, amazing visions and dreams, and prophetic scenarios that weave a visual history of redemption's saga. One might conclude from a study of both Old and New Testaments that Holy Scripture teaches the reality of the phrase "seeing is believing." The Bible describes, often in detailed descriptions, the tabernacle in the wilderness, the architecture of the temple, various individuals, groups of people, battles, events of celebration, and types of catastrophic events. Biblically described events are often singular and unique, primarily unknown to the human eye. For example, a burning bush, a chariot of fire, angelic beings: these and countless other instances reveal the intense visuality of the biblical text. The Bible describes human journeys of faith: God's relationship with his creation and created ones: the history of the people of God. These realities are vividly presented, with illustrative prose and poetry evoking a reader to "see" images of the persons, places, and events described.

The Bible is, from Genesis to Revelation, a feast of visual images. The knowledge of Old Testament prophets was often discerned through visual perception: God revealing particular visions portraying important meanings to be shared with God's people. The canon of Scripture, both the Hebrew Bible and the New Testament, contains countless descriptive visual images, replete with great detail. For example, a few of these descriptive images include the tabernacle in the wilderness, the description of the priests' garments, the prophetic visions of Jeremiah, Ezekiel, and other prophets, the stunning description of Christ's passion, Jesus revealing his wounds to Thomas, and the mysterious and profoundly moving visual images of the Revelation of St. John. The reception of knowledge and wisdom from God, as received by faith, is described biblically and throughout Christian history by phases such as "seeing the light," "seeing the truth," "having one's eyes open to truth," and so forth.

"Seeing" in one's imagination the images described in Scripture contrasts with Hellenistic or Western ways of thinking which deal with theological ideas in conceptual, intellectual terms. As Robby Gallaty explains, Hebraic thinking is comfortable dealing with theological concepts in tension.[1] Traditionally, the Jewish people preferred

> . . . word pictures, stories, poetry, imagery, and symbolism to the 'Western' or 'Greek' preference for words, ideas, definitions, outlines, lists and bullet points. The goal is not simply to resolve a problem or arrive at a conclusion. When a rabbi tells a story, he speaks to the heart first and the head second. Traditionally, Western ways of thinking tend to speak to the head first and the heart second.[2]

For example, Hellenistic or Western historical linguistics would answer the question "What is God?" by conceptual, intellectual terms: "God is love, God is merciful, God is holy." Although these conceptual terms appear in Scripture, there are numerous descriptions of God using terms that are vivid, visual, and common: "God is our Hightower; God is our Rock; I Am Living Water; I Am the Bread of Life."[3] These terms reveal truth by

1. Gallaty, *Rediscovering Discipleship*, 44.
2. Gallaty, *Rediscovering Discipleship*, 44.
3. Gallaty, *Rediscovering Discipleship*, 44–45.

using simple, mundane terms, understandable to people's experience and relatable to their understanding of life and to their emotional sensibilities. Because visual works of art often express truth in symbolic ways, artistic vision and expression are relatable to the visual realities of biblical Hebrew, and thus the use of art in spiritual direction supports one's need to understand and engage with theological truth.

Countless works of art throughout history reference biblical events and the eschatological reality of events to come. For the saints whose lives were chronicled in the Bible, seeing was truly believing. John refers to the reality of faith in Jesus Christ experienced through his fellow apostles' physical senses: "What was from the beginning, what we have heard, what we have seen with our eyes, what we have looked at and touched with our hands, concerning the Word of Life and the life was manifested, and we have seen and testify and proclaim to you the eternal life, which was with the Father and was manifested to us. . . ." [4] John's declaration emphasizes that the apostles' experience of Christ's reality was not merely intellectual, or only a deeply mysterious, spiritual relationship. Although the actual physical presence of Jesus was not possible after his ascension, the reality of God's truth can be perceived through the mediated communication of the arts.

Visions of Truth

Vision is a primary physical sense through which God reveals truth. The Holy Spirit may speak, guide, and direct through the physical senses. The Lord appeared to his people in physical form, as the incarnate Son. He died physically, arose from the grave physically, and ascended to heaven physically. The realities of his death, resurrection, and ascension were witnessed visually by others. There are those who dismiss the importance of the physical senses to spiritual life and growth. However, the biblical record and post-biblical history give witness to the importance of visual, tactile, and auditory senses in the development of individual and community spirituality. By the use of art in spiritual direction, knowledge of God, self, and others often increase, stimulating an individual's growth in faith that first emerges as a vision of truth.

4. 1 John 1: 1–2 NASB.

Images of Prophetic Reality

Artistic works sometimes serve to reveal a form of prophetic reality, providing a context for clarity in seeking that which is real and true. The prophets, those visionaries of the Old Testament, may be compared, in some aspects, with today's spiritual directors. Both prophets and spiritual directors are required to understand the power of vision; the power in discerning God's voice and sharing what is discerned with appropriate others, to achieve redemptive purposes in people's lives.

In studying and meditating on Old Testament books, visual aspects of both didactic and narrative passages emerge as images in the mind of the reader. These visual images, relative to people, places, and events in the context of biblical history, portray common themes in life and faith, helping individuals connect with similar experiences and emotional dimensions in their own lives. For example, the Old Testament narratives depicting soldiers in battle may help individuals relate to events in their own lives or the lives of relatives or friends who have experienced military service on the battlefield.

The Prophetic Dimension of Spiritual Direction

In Scripture, the prophetic is revealed in two dimensions. The prophets or seers foretold the will of God, foreshadowing future events and often forewarning people concerning the eventualities that would occur if they continued pursuing plans or actions that were disobedient in following God's will. Forthtelling is the ministry of proclamation: to tell forth the truth of God, primarily the good news of God's salvation, possible through Jesus Christ for all people. Prophetic reality is a constant in both the Old and New Testament writings. The prophetic speaks to the inner person. It is redemptive for the purposes ordained by God to inform and shape a person's life, their growth, development, and their formational spirituality in Christ.

The prophetic may be revealed through spoken or written words, through music, through the visual arts such as painting and drawing, the three-dimensional arts of sculpture and textiles, the art of the dance, and other artistic expressions. The prophetic in life and in art has redemptive purposes: a painting portraying Christ's crucifixion forthtells the reality of John's proclamation: "For God so loved the world, that He gave His only begotten Son, that whoever believes in Him shall not perish, but have eternal life."[5] The proclamation of truth through the medium of art applies to all art forms. For example, the *Pietá*, sculpted in marble by Michelangelo, forthtells the reality of Christ's death and portrays Mary's mourning as she beholds the death of her Son. In music, Handel's *Messiah* forthtells the reality of Jesus Christ in history and throughout eternity.

Pietà, Michelangelo

Spiritual direction is a ministry with prophetic dimensions in the sense that direction attempts to assist the directee in discerning the movements, guidance, and voice of the Holy Spirit relative to the entirety of one's faith and life. For example, the Spirit may reveal a sense of one's vocation: God's call to loving service, both present and future. Or the Spirit may simply affirm the reality of the gospel's relevance to one's life and ministry. Therefore, both foretelling and forthtelling are aspects of the prophetic that

5. John 3:16 NASB.

may emerge through visions of truth in spiritual direction as revealed by artistic expressions.

For the Old Testament prophet as well as the modern spiritual director, vision derives not only from physical sight, but from those visions that appear to one's inner, spiritual sight as revealed by the Holy Spirit. Visions related to the use of art in spiritual direction are multifaceted. A work of art, whether purely visual, or auditory, or having kinesthetic characteristics, will have countless meanings depending on an individual's interpretation of the artwork. For example, a portrayal of the Crucifixion, in any genre of art, may speak one message to those without faith in Christ and a different message to those who know Jesus Christ as Savior and Lord. Although a particular work of art may initially appear to the spiritual director as one-dimensional and limited in the sense of the truth it evokes, the director may be surprised to discover that the work of art evokes multiple layers of meanings, both spiritually and emotionally relevant to the individual engaged in the process. Therefore, art has no limitation when the director is committed to the guidance and revelation of the Holy Spirit's presence within the process of using art in spiritual direction.

ARTISTIC FORMS AND SPIRITUAL TRUTH

Historically and contemporarily, artistic forms have often served as visual revealers and reminders of spiritual truth.

> From the standpoint of the arts minister, there are several important points to be made here. In the course of salvation history, God discloses something of the character and mystery of divine presence to human beings. We respond to this revelation in a number of distinctive ways, among which is our artistry. On the one hand, the art that is produced is ultimately a result of the gifts and inspiration first provided by God. On the other hand, this same art also serves as a medium through which God's presence is unveiled before our very eyes. It shows us that which was hidden both in the divine and human sphere. Revelation is not mechanical or under the control of the artist. It is a gift of grace.[6]

Throughout the age of Christianity great works of art have continued to provide revelations of truth and symbols of spiritual beauty and reality in the experience of human life, as revealed by God through the symbolic

6. Bauer, *Arts Ministry*, 68.

relevance of these works. For example, Michelangelo's profoundly moving frescoes on the Sistine Chapel ceiling of the Vatican in Rome provide visions of truth that are timeless, These masterpieces representing high Renaissance art continue to inspire their viewers. Rembrandt van Rijn, the Dutch master, is known for his prolific works depicting individuals and events drawn from biblical history. His paintings of *Christ Appearing to Mary Magdalen, Christ Before Pilate, Peter Denying Christ,* and *The Raising of the Cross and The Raising of Lazarus* are among the works created by this master of the Renaissance period.

These and countless other works of art, in various media and genres, are often created by artists deeply committed to expressing spiritual reality and vitality in their works, drawing from their own everyday culture and people to create art, the realism of which allows the viewer to relate to an artist's message:

> Rembrandt used local Jews as his models for biblical characters. He used street people as well, and the model for one of his paintings of King Solomon was a local baker. While some artists depicted biblical characters as remote and superhuman figures, Rembrandt made them look like real people, on the assumption that the people of the Bible where flesh and blood just as his models were. He could, it seems, see into his own soul, just as he saw into the souls of the people of the Bible and could bring them to life on canvas. In at least one painting, *The Raising of the Cross,* he included himself in the picture as one of the Roman soldiers raising the cross of Jesus, his admission that he, like all human beings, was responsible for the death of Christ.[7]

7. Lang, *Christian History Devotional*, 206.

The Raising of the Cross, Rembrandt van Rijn

When an artist in any medium is creating works that are not only relative to the Christian faith but expressed by an artist who lives that faith, there is an undeniable authenticity, vitality, and power to the artwork. The message of the art, its very substance and meaning, is consonant with the faith of one engaged in spiritual direction. If the directee is not yet a person of faith but in search of knowing God, the artist's own commitment to Christ as expressed in the art's message results in a vision of truth that cannot help but impact the beholder of the work. In these instances, the artwork serves as a witness to the reality of God.

Artistic Images: Speaking to Faith and Culture

Images, depictions, or various symbolisms depicted in diverse forms of art have the power to impact not only individuals but entire groups, even nations of people. Although attributed to supernatural means, and not by the creation of the human artist, *Our Lady of Guadalupe*, a representation of the Virgin Mary in which her physical features resemble those of the Mexican people, is the most attended Marian shrine existing in the world. The image has also been adopted as heavenly patroness of the Philippines, indicating the power of the image to emotionally and spiritually connect those of Catholic faith with a primary religious figure of their faith. As one learns from this example, it is possible for art to speak to identity and the collective consciousness of a family, a group, or even a nation. The age of a work of art, and the artistic style of the era in which it was created, does not diminish the impact of the artwork and its influence as a means to spiritual understanding in the life of an individual or collective lives of a group. Common truths, common themes, and common aspects of faith and life are found across the ages in diverse forms of art.

Our Lady of Guadalupe

Making Sensitive Decisions in Selecting Works of Art

The wise director will research art forms and specific examples of artworks that are appropriate choices for a particular person's journey in spiritual direction. Choices should take into account the directee's faith tradition and other factors important to consider in choosing works of art for use in direction. Without the director's sensitivity in the process of choosing art forms and particular examples of art, the directee may experience cognitive, emotional, and/or spiritual dissonance with the direction experience, because the art chosen does not resonate with the person's life and sense of spiritual reality. On the other hand, a director may use art forms or specific examples of art that do not initially appear integrated with an individual's spiritual experience yet, upon exploration, the person may discover the artwork's subjects and meanings speak in new ways concerning their experiences, feelings, spiritual hopes, and longings. For example, a person from the millennial generation may feel far removed from the style and meanings of religious sculptures at the Royal Portal of the Chartres Cathedral (twelfth century), yet reflection on the work—what it represents spiritually and emotionally—may become meaningful even to someone so far removed from that era's artistic sensitivities and styles. Although the uniqueness of each individual in the ministry of direction should be considered and respected, there is also the importance of remaining open to the Holy Spirit's leading, trusting that a prayerful director will have discernment in choosing those works of art that become meaningful and valuable to each directee's life and faith experience.

Royal Portal of the Chartres Cathedral

The use of art in spiritual direction requires the director's sense of creativity to understand how a particular work of art may be used to enhance the process of direction, becoming a resource to encourage a directee's spiritual growth. Direction requires a basic understanding of the meaning and value of art forms to one's spirituality, and ways in which these art forms may be applied to one's journey in the ministry of spiritual direction. Individual choices of artwork are literally endless, therefore, the director has to choose the type of art form and the particular uses of that form: how a specific work of art will best enhance the directee's experience in spiritual discernment and formation.

The director should first become familiar with the use of art forms in his or her own directorial experience, under the guidance of a qualified spiritual direction supervisor. This process will provide the knowledge and training to help the director avoid using a ministry resource in which he or she has no previous experience. Schools and training centers for spiritual directors may enlarge and enrich their programs and better serve their students by providing education and training in the use of art in spiritual direction.

The Family: Revealed in Art

One of the most powerful and evocative art forms for use in spiritual direction is photography. Many families retain a photographic history of their lives extending over time. Often family history is recorded in still photography, film, or video media. These images have important uses not only in the ministry of spiritual direction, but also in counseling and therapeutic settings to address emotional needs. Even a simple drawing or an artistically embellished version of a family tree, listing family members over the period of several generations, have power to evoke thoughts, memories, reflections, and insights important to continuing spiritual growth and maturing relationships with God, family, community, and others. Textile art, for example, as created in a quilt crafted by one's mother, grandmother, or other family member, reveals something about the values and character of the quilter to the person reflecting on the art of the quilt.

Family symbols expressed in various works of art speak of genealogy, identity, nurture, and love, as well as emotional and spiritual connections with family members. These works often reveal the unfolding thread of religious sensibilities and practices of faith in a particular family. Textile artistry, for example, as seen in a baptismal gown, first Communion dress, wedding gown, and other articles of clothing, perhaps lovingly hand-created and worn only on special occasions, often stimulate memories connected to each piece of clothing and evoke reflections on the meaning of these occasions to one's spiritual life. Favorite musical forms and particular pieces of music common to a family's life experience can quickly evoke memories and produce a response.

Adding Value and Depth to Spiritual Direction

As the spiritual director employs music, textile art, painting, sculpture, or other art forms in spiritual direction sessions, he or she brings additional dimensions of depth and truth to the ministry of spiritual formation. All art forms have the potential to be used in spiritual direction when appropriate in helping individuals prayerfully reflect on their spiritual history: their journey in faith and how that journey has been shaped and molded within the person's family context and also in the context of other relationships. Works of art which do not specifically depict religious subjects may, in view of their overall meaning, be used by the Holy Spirit to affirm God's love and care or stimulate spiritual awakenings or knowledge necessary to one's spiritual growth. As James McCullough explains,

> While works of art cannot and should not be reduced to singular detachable 'messages', artworks always communicate some sense of life, a perspective on things. It is in attending with some greater sensitivity and openness to this communicative dynamic at the heart of art that I maintain spiritual formation can actually take place.[8]

The process of engagement and reflection in the ministry of spiritual direction includes time set aside to engage with a particular work of art in painting, sculpture, music, textiles, and other art forms, including dramatic presentations. Allowing this process of engagement, including quietness and reflection, stimulates the emergence of memories, ideas, insights, and emotions related to one's person's life and continuing spiritual progress. Even qualities such as color, texture, lighting, visual depth, and other characteristics of art in paintings, textiles, sculptures, etc., may evoke responses relating to personal spirituality. The uses of art in spiritual direction are

8. McCullough, xvii.

limitless; their diversity and applications emphasize the creativity of art's uses by the inspiration of Holy Spirit, who is always understood as the true director.

Art: Values Ancient and New

Human history includes common themes spiritually, intellectually, emotionally, and relationally. These common themes may speak authentically to individuals far removed from the era in which the particular art form was created. In fact, it is often true that the art of an earlier age speaks to individuals in ways that exceed the artistic voices of works created in the present age. There are particular areas of spiritual blindness in every age; therefore, in viewing artistic works from an earlier age, one is lifted from spiritual apathy or from an inability to discern certain dimensions of spirituality. To begin to discern the reality of God as understood in a former age opens new vistas of knowledge and understanding applicable to many aspects of one's life. In spiritual direction, using several art forms, including specific pieces that span a long historical progression, provides variety to help individuals understand the ways art expresses the unlimited qualities of authentic spirituality.

The age of an artistic work does not limit the possibilities of its use. A work of art created in a past era retains the possibility to reveal volumes of truth to those who carefully consider its message. Due to the uniqueness of each individual, one person may spiritually resonate with the truth depicted in a work of art that is centuries old, whereas another person may be drawn to modern or contemporary works. Older works often become classics, revered due to their artistry, subject matter, and meaning. Contemporary works of art are created every day and therefore provide new ways to express truth and provide limitless options for the use of art in spiritual direction.

Using Art with Care

Any work of art is open to highly subjective individual interpretations. It is not uncommon for persons visiting art galleries to stand or sit near a particular work of art and while gazing at the work, reflect on its meaning, both generally and as the artwork relates to very personal aspects of the viewer's life. The well-prepared spiritual director will use all forms of art with much care, helping to guide and support an individual's spiritual awareness by using works of art in ways that are wholly beneficial to the direction process.

To Explore the Seen and Unseen

Often, we find our character, abilities, and lives in general interpreted through the eyes of others. However, art itself can serve as a mirror to reflect true aspects of the inner self, including the nature of one's relationships with God, ourselves, and others. Art brings us to a place of encountering ourselves and others, of beginning to understand the process of spiritual maturity. The appropriate use of art provides new understandings, often about personal needs including woundedness, that eventually lead to healing one's misconceptions, even one's blindness to the true nature of life, God, the self, and others. It is not an artwork in itself that unveils truths, but rather the presence of the Holy Spirit whose truth is revealed through the mediated communication of art as one prayerfully reflects, prays, discusses, and embraces what one is thinking, feeling, seeing, or hearing from an encounter with art.

The total reality and meaning of each person's life is hidden, partially known to the self but fully known to God. Much of what one knows about the self is rarely spoken or discussed. Inward truths are often repressed or not known to the conscious mind. Experiencing art often unveils hidden parts of our lives, uncovering them in the presence of God, and making one aware of truths previously unknown or not understood. The daily flow of life, with its busyness, responsibilities, changes, conflicts, and stresses, tends to cause the hiding or repression of truth so important to one's spiritual vitality and growth. Encounters with art have the potential to open the locked doors of personal truth. With the help of the spiritual director, these unlocked vistas of truth are open to further exploration, resulting in a fuller realization and understanding of one's relationship with God, ourselves, and others.

Art forms may be implemented to explore the meaning and value of what is both thought and seen, heard and touched, as well as those things discerned through spiritual vision: the reality that is often perceived inwardly, and points to spiritual truth. Humanity lives in a three-dimensional world. Dimensions existing beyond the earthly realm can only be experienced through spiritual vision: the inward reality of God's truth as revealed by the Holy Spirit. The Bible describes people living in a three-dimensional world and yet experiencing a fourth or perhaps other unknown dimensions only accessible and understandable through authentic spiritual vision. Art forms have the potential, through the guidance of the Holy Spirit, to encourage an individual to pursue the dimension of faith: "Now faith is the assurance of things hoped for the conviction of things not seen."[9] Art is more visual, tactile, or auditory, depending on genre, than the written word. Therefore, art has the ability to reveal truth in wordless ways, often on deeply emotional and spiritual levels that cannot be accessed through intellectual understanding alone. One must discover one's inward voice, the voice of one's spirit, as aligned with the indwelling Holy Spirit, to express one's praise, worship, and prayers to God. The use of art in spiritual direction provides a way for directees to express that hidden or repressed self that, waiting in silence, has not yet found the courage or the words and emotional openness to allow one's voice to emerge. Art provides a way to encourage one's inner voice, and through the Holy Spirit, to free that voice to express the inner self to God. One of the greatest needs in prayer is to know and express one's innermost self to God. Doing so is an important part in understanding one's relationship to God. In expressing the authentic voice of one's spirit through prayer, one joins in the dance of continual discovery and joy in the Lord.

As in any process where subjectivity is a factor, it cannot be overstated that the discernment expressed by someone in the context of spiritual direction must include a high accountability factor in that what the directee shares should be evaluated to determine if it aligns with biblical truth. As previously stated, it is understood that the true director, in the context of spiritual direction in the Christian tradition, is always understood as the Holy Spirit. Therefore, when one expresses one's own sense of inner truth, a director has the responsibility to assist a directee to understand if the thoughts and ideas shared agree with an orthodox understanding of scriptural reality. Christian spiritual direction must always maintain a high view of and commitment to the biblical canon. Spiritual directors must be careful not to consider any type of subjective experience or personal discernment of equal or higher importance than holy Scripture.

Art, due to its nature and uses, sets one free from the limitations often evident in interactive dialogue or discussion. Added to dialogue and discussion in spiritual direction, art encourages the discernment of spiritual

9. Heb 11:1 NASB.

realities that are vitally important to growth in Christ. Spiritual direction is a process involving both teaching and learning' therefore, additional tools and resources, such as a variety of art forms, greatly enhance the meaning and value of the ministry.

Discerning the Movements of the Holy Spirit

It is not uncommon in spiritual direction for individuals to struggle in the process of learning to discern the movements of the Holy Spirit, to clarify and understand those movements as they pertain to one's life. The use of art in spiritual direction has the potential to bring focus and clarity to important spiritual issues. The proper use of art resources may help the directee focus on thoughts, emotions, and feelings not expressed or understood due to life experiences of hurt, trauma, or fear.

One of the potential benefits of spiritual direction is to resolve an individual's sense of isolation from others including the feeling of remoteness in one's quest for relationship with God. The use of art in direction may help an individual emerge from feelings of emotional isolation, the sense that "I'm the only one who thinks or feels this way." An artistic creation draws the beholder of the art into the idea or experience the artist's work expresses. The use of art allows an important connection with others, with the artist as well as with those who find value in the art, especially in a work's ability to evoke memories of people's common life experiences. As with the use of religious icons, art is meant not simply to draw one merely to the dimensions of the work of art itself, but to draw the individual beyond the work's immediate meaning, to the dimension of God's reality. Therefore, a work of art can fulfill holy purposes in one's life of faith, serving as a lens, a mirror, a pathway, or an opening to understanding a greater reality as one considers a work of art in the light of Scripture. As Jem Sullivan explains,

> The creation of sacred art can be considered in some sense a holy act. For a painting's pigment or a sculpture's shape is the beginning of a dialogue where the spiritual contemplation of one person—the artist—is set forth in such a fashion as to provoke the beginning of the viewer's contemplation. Consequently, we cannot overestimate its capacity to become [according to Pope Benedict XVI] 'a place to encounter the living God who in Jesus Christ reveals his transforming love and truth'[10]

10. Sullivan, *Beauty of Faith*, 12.

Overcoming limitations

Another important example of how the use of art in spiritual direction can affect one's spiritual vision in the inward and private thoughts of the heart relates to those who are vision impaired. Having the opportunity to touch and to explore a piece of sculpture, or feel the surface of a painting or the fibers of textile art, may open doors of discovery and understanding which discussion alone with the spiritual director will not accomplish. Another example is spiritual direction with the hearing impaired or deaf. Direction in this context may be enriched by the use of art forms which provide a powerful context for the deaf to encounter new spiritual meanings in life and faith; ways in which they recognize the communication of God mediated through art as they listen inwardly with heart and spirit.

The Power of Symbol

One can never underestimate the power of symbol, including the many symbols contained within the pages of Scripture and the countless meaningful emblems one encounters every day and throughout all of life. Often the meaning of symbols, perhaps one as ubiquitous as a wedding band for example, may be overlooked and not reflected upon within the busyness of daily life. Symbols are instrumental as reminders of actual reality. Focusing on a wooden cross, for example, encourages reflection on the reality of Christ's sacrifice and his completed work of redemption.

Art provides limitless opportunities to engage in reflection and listen for the voice of the Holy Spirit speaking clearly as one reflects on the meaning and value of a particular symbol. Reflection upon appropriate symbols, including works of art, assists individuals in becoming more open to movements of the Holy Spirit working in our lives and speaking to our hearts throughout the many moments within each day. For those who have the capacity to view symbols with the eyes, or for the visually impaired who "see" through touch or verbal descriptions, the power and meaning of symbols must not be underestimated as to their importance in spiritual direction and in the whole of one's spiritual life. Setting aside, within the hours of the day, a few moments for reflection and prayer related to a particular symbol invites the Spirit's presence and encourages quiet contemplation concerning the important questions of life and faith.

Such moments of grace may make all the difference in one's daily progress and growth in spiritual maturity. The following are questions helpful to use in the process of reflecting on symbolic meanings during sessions of spiritual direction: In what ways is the symbol important to me? Does the symbol occur in Scripture? If so, what is its possible meaning? Does the symbol have contemporary meaning? Is God speaking to me now through this symbol? Is the reality this symbol represents calling me to a particular action in prayer or in service to God and to others?

Disciplines Enhancing Artistic Awareness

For those with busy lives, there is often the tendency to hide from one's true self, to avoid exploring one's nature and the quality of one's relationship with God and others, as well as avoiding attentiveness to the overarching spiritual needs of life. Encounters with art through the ministry of spiritual direction demand that one slow down, practice the disciplines of quietness, reflection, and prayer, and devote the time needed to fully engage with a work of art. It is through slowing down, reflective silence, contemplation, and conversational sharing that art's message is revealed as meaningful and valuable to the one engaged with the artwork. One may forget a conversation, but it is difficult to erase visual and auditory memories from one's mind. These symbols may be remembered again and again to recall the Holy Spirit's message imparted through encounters with art.

ARCHITECTURE AND ART: HOLY PLACES, SACRED SPACES

The great basilicas, cathedrals, and churches throughout history display stunning architecture and contain works of art providing visual as well as tactile representations of biblical events and Christian themes. Places and spaces carefully designed to announce messages of truth speak eloquently to the lives of those who worship within them. The physical senses, spiritual discernment, and the yearning for beauty in one's life point to the inward desire to explore and express what is real and meaningful in one's lived expressions of faith. Art provides a way of mediated communication for the purpose of giving expression to life and faith and therefore should not be ignored.

> Christians, after all, believe humans are created in the image and likeness of God and that creation was lovingly and artfully shaped by the hand of God. Humans, therefore, even in their fallen condition, are capable of making worthy arts. God as creator and sustainer still holds the world in his hands. Christ, moreover, rules culture as the risen and ascended Lord. These facts alone should stimulate Christians to be concerned with the visual dimension of life and the power of images that surround them. And of all the images that matter, those that serve as the personal expression of artists, whether Christian or not, should concern us most deeply.[11]

Until the time in history when the invention of the printing press allowed dissemination of the biblical texts, Christians depended upon the soaring spaces of cathedrals, the grandeur of sun-filled stained glass windows, the sculptures of biblical figures, and the paintings of biblical themes representing past, present, and future to serve as teachers, spiritual directors, and doorways to prayer and reflection on the holy. These places and spaces for worship, so unlike the humble dwellings of common people, allowed worshipers to experience the numinous and yet remain grounded by Christ's teaching to love God and love neighbors. Throughout history people have struggled daily to deal with life's problems and traumas, both personal and societal, including realities of war, death, and natural disasters. The church, with its visual beauty and symbols pointing to the assurance of God's presence and love, became a refuge of grace and relief from the often overwhelming challenges of everyday life.

In a cathedral or more modest church edifice, one worshiped with physical feet planted on the ground while one's spirit could soar to heavenly places in Christ Jesus. Therefore, art created for a community of faith in which each individual met to worship, complemented the sanctuary and other holy spaces, witnessing to worshipers' spirits the reality of God's majesty, the beauty of God's holiness, and the eternal life to come for those who believed. Artistic forms in worship places and spaces were silent yet profoundly moving symbols and forms that drew many worshipers to desire God's presence, to know the reality of Divinity in the midst of lives fraught with daily, often severe difficulties. The church, with its otherworldly beauty, made real the presence of God, for surely such beauty could not exist unless God was real and present with his people. The music of the worshiping community complemented the silent art forms of holy spaces

11. Dyrness, *Visual Faith*, 20.

and places, integrating all the created forms of art, architecture, textiles, and music into one harmonious whole built for the glory of God and calling God's people together in worship. The beauty of basilicas, cathedrals, and churches reminded believers that no matter what difficulties life may hold outside the doors that opened into places of worship, the church's holy spaces of otherworldly beauty gave witness to the reality of God's presence and promises to his people.

In historical eras when the vicissitudes of life including poverty, disease, wars, slavery, early death, and other realities made day to day living a constant struggle, a cathedral or many churches with their soaring arches, massive stained-glass windows, inlaid woods, precious stones, sculptures, and rich textiles gave entrance for the common man and woman to a world that spoke eloquently on earth of heaven and the joys of eternal life. Even a relatively humble church had its symbols of artistic beauty, its very existence forming a centerpiece, a focal point, both physical and spiritual, for the worshiping community's life and purpose. Every commoner may not have a spiritual director, but the beautiful artistic forms of the community's church served as silent prophets, pointing one's life to the truth and beauty of God. Artistic works provided encouragement to follow the pilgrim way of daily faith. In contemporary society, which overflows with visual stimulation through technology and provides access to view diverse forms of art, experiencing artistic works common to Christian worship is available to a much wider global audience than in previous eras. One may choose to virtually tour the great cathedrals of Europe on television, computer, phone, or other media. Many also have access, as never before, to travel the world and experience the diversity of the arts, an impossibility for most individuals in former centuries.

Art in Community: Historical and Contemporary Examples

There are many historical and contemporary examples of the ways in which art helps to form, unify, and sustain a particular community. A well-known example is the work of Renaissance artist Michelangelo di Lodovico Buonarroti Simoni, in particular the frescoes painted on the ceiling of the Vatican's Sistine Chapel.[12] His magnificent frescoes, although contained in the

12. The Sistine Chapel was built during the papacy of Sixtus IV, and the frescoes were commissioned by Julius II and completed in the period between 1508–1512. Michelangelo's representational painting *The Last Judgment* appears on the chapel's sanctuary wall.

context of the Roman Catholic community, speak powerfully and eloquently of the entirety of the Christian faith's shared truths. The ceiling frescoes and other art in the Sistine Chapel remain as major works, their artistic power and beauty enduring for centuries. Any work of art contained in a worship space, and visible to the worshiping community, remains important on many levels to the spiritual life of a congregation. For example, even informal photographs of community events in a local church serve as artistic representations of the shared faith and life of that community. They provide a visual history of important events and remembrances of people in the community, those who are presently members, and those who may no longer be members or have passed away, and are remembered as beloved participants in that community.

Sistine Chapel, the Vatican

Creating a Shared Spiritual Identity

The Old Testament tabernacle in the wilderness, and later the temple, were created with careful attention to the Lord's instructions explaining the materials to use and the precise ways to build each edifice and article needed for the religious life of the community. Every individual part and piece of furniture in the tabernacle and temple symbolized spiritual realities. God's people formed an identity through specific practices of worship which drew them to the reality of God's presence with the community. The architecture and artistically designed symbols of the Jewish faith served to foster not only a sense of identity but of unity as a people. The power of visual images which have shared meaning cannot be underestimated in their ability to create and sustain a sense of community and the people's perspective concerning their past, present, and future in their Lord.

Art, when appropriately used, has the ability to help new members integrate into the shared spiritual journey of a faith community. In exploring the art forms that are part of any community, one may learn the history of the congregation. This process engenders both an individual member's and the corporate body's greater sense of belonging. The types of art included in a community context also encourage new members to consider the ways in which they may bring their own particular expressions of artistic giftings to a community.

One may have different responses to works of art that exist in worship spaces, depending on the life event an individual or family is experiencing at any particular time. For example, stained glass windows may speak silently yet eloquently throughout one's life but reveal deeper layers of meaning depending on a person's particular season of life and the specific events related to that season.

The art and architecture of places and spaces for worship become integral parts of a community's worship life. A wooden cross, a clerestory window, the sculpture of a religious scene, the design of the sanctuary, the paraments, furniture, and liturgical vessels become part of the worshiping community's interactive response to the presence of God. As people enter and participate in the fellowship and worship life of community, they carry with them, in hearts and minds, the joy and strength of shared worship. The visual remembrances, the emotional memories of words and music, and all that is experienced through the use of the arts in a worship space, enrich each person's life and the collective life of a faith community.

Architecture, sculpture, textiles, music, photography, and other artistic forms are often used to encourage spiritual connectedness to one's faith community. Art that endures, often existing and providing inspiration and enjoyment for several generations of a worshiping community, creates the reality of shared experience just as the experience of art in an individual family creates a similar sense of shared experience among the members. Art may be used to encourage a common identity among community members because the place of worship becomes a shared spiritual home for individuals, families, and the corporate faith community. This connectedness to past generations, to the present community, and to future generations is made stronger through the shared experiences provided by artistic forms. The contemporary church in many global contexts is experiencing resurgence in the use of diverse artistic media as part of worship:

> In churches, especially fast-growing charismatic and megachurches, visual and dramatic arts are becoming a standard part of worship. Special effects, dramatic skits, movie clips, slides of artwork, to say nothing of worship bands, are common in "contemporary" worship services. While some may doubt whether these works and compositions will stand the test of time, or whether they are contributing to truly biblical worship, clearly there is creative energy—and excitement—here.[13]

Stewardship of Spiritual Symbols

Caring for the architecture and art of a worship space is a privilege of life in community. It is often in the acts of providing stewardship for these precious elements of community life that one's own spirituality is enriched. As faith matures, one understands more clearly the need for symbols, their meaning, power, and the necessity for their care and preservation throughout the life of a church.

Art in Community and Spiritual Direction

One of the most important aspects of the spiritual direction process is the ministry's ability to encourage and assist an individual's growth in relationships within the believer's faith community context. In every community

13. Dyrness, *Visual Faith*, 14.

of believers there are shared joys, griefs, relational conflicts, and perhaps traumatic events. The use of art in spiritual direction allows the individual to explore his or her past and present experiences in community and to prayerfully consider plans for spiritual growth in the context of continuing relationships with others.

When art is used in spiritual direction, directors must understand that each person has inter and intra-aspects of relationship and communication in one's life. Spiritual direction concerns the believer's relationship with God as well as one's relationships with faith community members and individuals and groups outside the community. Engaging with art in spiritual direction provides a way to explore and find meaning in both individual and corporate relational dimensions. Using art also concerns the dimension of the mystery of God, the unknown yet real aspects of one's present and eternal life with Deity. These dimensions are interwoven in one's life, integrated as one seeks to live life with God, self, and others in a spirit of truth.

If an individual receiving direction has particular art forms common to his or her faith community, then encouraging prayerful reflection on these symbols and their meanings to the individual's past, present, and future faith journey is an excellent way to encourage one's understanding of the personal significance of these art forms. Worshiping communities develop a shared visual sense, as individuals join together in the same holy spaces for worship, week after week, and year after year, as a corporate body. Members of the community view these places and spaces for worship as their spiritual family's home, for these designated areas are the common meeting places in which fellowship is shared, faith strengthened, and vision for ministry and mission emerges. The physical "church home" as it is sometimes called, encourages a sense of being present in the community's spiritual center, when each member of the congregation joins with others in worship.

In the process of spiritual direction, it is important for participants to have opportunities to contemplate and to discuss their thoughts and emotional responses as related to the contained artworks of one's faith community. Works of art contained inside or outside a place of worship remain as artistic constants throughout members' many spiritual events: baptism, Eucharist, confirmation, marriage, funerals, and other hallmark events common to members and their families in a worshiping community. Various forms of art are present and important to all the events and the emotions that concern life in community. Art speaks to these shared events and emotions, representing many realities of faith which serve as constant reminders of God's loving presence, while encouraging the community's focus on eternal spiritual realities.[14] A baptismal font, sculpted in wood, metal, or stone; the pottery or metal of chalice and paten for Eucharist; the rich patterned fabrics of blue, purple, red, white, or green for vestments and paraments representing the liturgical seasons: these witness to eternal truths of the Christian faith. Each item is an art form pointing to the sanctity of God's gifts, the otherness of worship, and the power and beauty of the holy as experienced in community.

Individuals receive a form of spiritual direction as they live daily the ongoing journey of faith with their congregational community. In fellowship with other believers, the ministry of spiritual direction takes place on an informal but nonetheless valid basis. Through participation in worship, the Sacraments, Bible study, and other community events; through the sharing of individual and mutual joys and griefs; through partnering in ministry and mission, the community develops and matures in faith. Through all the experiences of one's faith community, Christians encounter a lived theology, those beliefs and practical actions that speak of authentic fellowship in Christ.

The Eloquence of Simplicity

In traditions where a faith community embraces a very simple yet eloquent style of worship, without vestments or artistic decoration, the visual power of simplicity becomes its own artistic form. Simplicity speaks visually to worshipers, pointing to the mystery of God, but also to the Lord's unseen yet very real presence with his people. Worship styles, ranging from the complex to the very simple, express a visual message and honor God's presence in diverse ways. Some spaces for worship contain little or no artistic representation but express simple practicality and frugality and therefore may be clean and spare in their design. These worship spaces, built for simple practicality, may contain few or no artistic works that speak overtly and symbolically of the Christian faith. Yet every edifice and its contents speak in some way about the purpose of place and space to those who enter for

14. "Set your mind on the things above, not on the things that are on earth. For you have died and your life is hidden with Christ in God. When Christ, who is our life, is revealed, then you also will be revealed with Him in glory" (Col 3:2–3, NASB).

worship. The more simply designed or sparsely decorated worship spaces are not limited in their ability to encourage both the individual's internal life of worship and the corporate body's outwardly expressed life of worship in community. Both simplicity of design and richness of art and decoration provide meaning to a congregation's worship life.

Informing One's Spiritual Journey

Aspects of artistic visuality inform one's journey of faith and serve to direct one's spirituality as relative to individual Christian traditions and the values and practices embracing faith within a tradition. The same principle is true concerning the use of art in spiritual direction. Some art forms are simple in design; other art forms are intricate and ornate. Regardless of style and expression, all art forms are able to communicate truth, each in its own way. Art is not limited in its message because of style or form but has many voices. Each one may express similar spiritual truths in unique and different ways. Renaissance art compared to contemporary art varies markedly in style, yet both forms may express truth to those who discern the meaning of the individual artist. Searching for personal truth in a diversity of art forms is often preferable to using only one artistic form, such as painting. However, using diverse forms and an overabundance of individual works of art may prove overwhelming for both the spiritual director and directee. An individual may experience the best results through engagement with a few simple yet sublime works of art that encourage reflection and prayer to achieve the goal of growth in one's spiritual life. Therefore, the wise director will be careful to gain knowledge of an individual's preferences; those types and examples of art that most resonate with the person's spiritual sensibilities.

Chapter 4

Uses of Art in Discerning God's Presence and Guidance

"Faith is the divine evidence whereby the spiritual man discerneth God, and the things of God."

—John Wesley, 1703–91

AESTHETIC PRESENCE

The use of visual images and auditory or physical expressions in artistic forms may serve to stimulate a directee's perception of God's presence, reveal evidence of God's guidance, or in general open new possibilities for embracing and understanding spiritual truth. The directee's responses to images and other artistic expressions may also assist the director in discerning a directee's need for referral to pastoral counseling or therapy. Artistic forms, due to their diversity, may be chosen by the director based on the directee's preferred style of learning and understanding: visual, auditory, or kinesthetic. A primary purpose for the use of art in direction is to provide aesthetic presence, visual stimulation, and a context for reflection, contemplation, and discernment, all of which are potential benefits when using various art forms. In spiritual direction art can provide the quality of aesthetic integrity by the inclusion of visual, auditory, and kinesthetic beauty. Aesthetics, appropriately used in spiritual direction, adds value and meaning in discerning and understanding one's inner spiritual life, prayer, relationships, and ministry. However, it is important to remember, when considering aesthetics in the use of art in spiritual direction, as Dietrich Hildebrand and Robert Wood assert: "Some things can only be approached with great reverence for it is only then that they disclose themselves to us as they truly are. One of those is beauty."[1] The authors opine that "Above all, beauty is a reflection of God, a reflection of his own infinite beauty, a genuine value, something that is important-in-itself, something that praises God." [2]

Art, as used in spiritual direction, uncovers new layers of meaning by allowing further exploration of a concept or a question. The meaning derived from an artistic work may come from the subject matter, or from the colorations, lighting, texture, shapes, materials, or other aesthetic aspects relating to the work.

Biblically, and in subsequent history, people of faith lived common lives where aesthetics in daily existence, for example the mundane routines of the home, were very simple or limited. Common persons often discovered their primary visible aesthetic reality in nature, which is not limited in its ability to inspire appreciation for God's gifts in the realm of earthly life. One's spirit hungers for the experience of worshiping God, allowing earthly symbols of beauty to inspire one to glorify the Lord in the beauty of his holiness.

The Meaning and Value of Aesthetics

In the process of spiritual direction it is important to consider the meaning and value of aesthetics. The visual beauty of worship is evident in many biblical descriptions of worship. The clothing used by priests, the vessels employed in the biblical tabernacle and temple, the materials, including gold and silver, various textiles, the use of space, and other visual elements, speak to worshipers of God's presence, beauty, power, and perfection of character. They speak also of the numinous quality of life, existing in earthly contexts, for in places and spaces for worship one encounters the Holy. Most worshipers, throughout the biblical era and in later history,

1. Von Hildebrand and Wood, *Aesthetics*, 1.
2. Von Hildebrand and Wood, *Aesthetics*, 2.

experienced common lives where aesthetics in daily life were nonexistent or limited. People of great wealth possessed the resources to create aesthetically pleasing spaces, homes, and palaces of great beauty, yet this was not the norm. The common person looked to God's gifts in the natural world—sky, trees, rivers, lakes, seas, and other aspects of creation—for examples of aesthetic reality. Engagement with and appreciation of the stunning beauty of the Lord's creation lifted one's spirit to God and encouraged worship. The human mind and spirit hungers for the beauty of God, for the joy found in attitudes and actions of worshiping God in the peerless beauty of his holiness. Even the poor, through nature and through the loveliness of worship spaces, experienced the reality of spiritual aesthetics.

Eighteenth century preacher, philosopher and theologian Jonathan Edwards maintains a viewpoint concerning beauty that may resonate with contemporary Christians. In *The Nature of True Virtue*,

> Edwards posits two types of beauty: primary and secondary. Primary beauty is true virtue, or spiritual beauty. Secondary beauty is what most people think of when they think of beauty, that is, physical beauty. For Edwards, physical beauty is a reflection in spiritual beauty or true virtue . . . something is beautiful in so far as it reflects or participates in true, spiritual beauty. For Edwards, of course, such primary beauty is grounded in the nature of God. Edwards' agenda in *The Nature of True Virtue* is similar (though not identical) [to Joseph D. Wooddell's view of spiritual aesthetics]. Edwards is a Christian who believes God might use beauty to draw a person to himself, and he is systematic in his treatment of the issue. Edwards sees both primary and secondary beauty as objective. . . .[3]

Wooddell argues that ". . . beauty is objective, not subjective . . ."[4] He posits that encountering beauty is not to be understood as a merely subjective experience. He understands that "something is beautiful in so far as it reflects the character, nature or will of God (all of which are unchanging)."[5] Wooddell understands that aesthetics and Christian apologetics are connected; therefore, "any Christian apologetic must not contradict Scripture, so discerning what Scripture has to say about beauty and apologetics is important."[6]

3. Wooddell, *Beauty of the Faith*, 46.
4. Wooddell, *Beauty of the Faith*, 47.
5. Wooddell, *Beauty of the Faith*, 47.
6. Wooddell, *Beauty of the Faith*, 59.

Encouraging Contemplation

In spiritual direction the inner, often unconscious yearning for beauty, can be acknowledged through the use of art. Not every work of art is considered aesthetically beautiful to everyone who views, touches, or hears the work. However, a work's meaning can have the potential to lift one's thoughts to what is beautiful. Even those works of art which do not initially resonate with one's aesthetic sensibilities have the potential to encourage the contemplation of God as he who is supremely beautiful in glory, in character, and in complete perfection of being. In art, the things of earth are often portrayed as objects that stimulate one's desire for the reality of heaven, for a relationship with God that is not only possible during earthly life but also promises the future fullness of eternal bliss in his presence. Art may encourage the contemplation of God's holy, sublime, and matchless beauty, and of those things on earth and in heaven that speak of beauty in all its forms.

Diverse Emotional Responses

A work of art may be aesthetically pleasing, expressing great beauty in subject, line, color, and composition, through which the artist expressed a reality or vision both valuable and meaningful in its content. However, an expression of joy and beauty is not always the subject of an art form. The use of art in spiritual direction may include the sublimely beautiful as well as subjects that are emotionally painful to behold. Art may present a subject expressing sadness, emotional pain, traumatic events, or other common human struggles. A work's theme may be war, poverty, despair, grief, hopelessness, or other conditions and emotions related to the artist's imagination, actual experiences, or to biblical, literary, or historic events. The beautiful and wonderful, as well as the most difficult realities of life, may serve to lift one's one spirit and one's thoughts toward God. Works of art with themes pointing to the hurt, struggles, and pain of sin in human life also have the power to stimulate faith, hope, and love as one considers the reality and presence of God: to whom else can one turn when face-to-face with the diverse realities of life?

The Importance of Aesthetics

The ability to understand and convey to others the reality of aesthetics and its importance to spiritual growth is essential for spiritual directors. It is important to consider the meaning and value of aesthetics to the believer. All that is beautiful, lovely, and sublime in one's life emerges from the true and the perfect, the ultimately most beautiful, who is God.

> The experience of worship—prayer, praise, and participation in the sacrament—provides for believers the opportunity of responding to the gracious presence of God with the whole of their beings. It is then embodied experience, involving standing, kneeling, or lifting of hands; it is a deeply emotional and intellectual response of the heart to God's offer of grace in Jesus Christ by the power of the Holy Spirit. But it is also an experience of the will as the believer gives up his or her life in service to God, by physically taking the bread and wine that is offered, or by going under the waters of baptism. Even such a brief description calls attention to the oral, visual, even kinesthetic dimensions of these experiences. These dimensions call for embodiment and performance that throughout Christian history have given birth to art. . . .[7]

The Yearning for Beauty

Engagement with works of art has the potential to encourage individuals to acknowledge their yearning to connect with the aesthetic aspects of life. It is not uncommon, due to sadness, grief, illness, or other losses which seem opposite to what is beautiful and joyful, that an individual may feel far removed from the aesthetics of life. The opportunity to see, touch, or hear those things which have the quality of beauty encourages spiritual understanding and assists in the processes of physical and emotional healing. Many people suffer from an unfulfilled yearning for beauty. They may not recognize or acknowledge their yearning. They may live from day to day desiring to see, feel, touch, or hear those things in life which are most beautiful and raise one's thoughts to contemplate the beauty of God. As Robert Mixa explains, beauty has a connection to the Christian spiritual life. Because beauty is discerned in many artistic works, then the use of art in spiritual direction can draw us to the reality of Jesus Christ.

> Since Christ is Love made visible and religious life is conformity to Christ, religious life is a continuation of that love made visible in Christ. Love is perfect, showing forth integrity. There is no lack. It is the perfection of all things. It is harmonious and proportionate.

7. Dyrness, *Visual Faith*, 22–23.

> It does not undermine . . . . The parts are united into a harmonious whole (order). Lastly, it shines forth. It communicates itself, bringing others into its life.
>
> If religious life is an intense participation in the Christ life, which is Love, it will meet these three criteria. In an age full of thrills but lacking in beauty, Dostoyevsky's prophecy that 'beauty will save the world' needs to be taken seriously. Taking into consideration what was said above, then it makes sense to say the beauty of the religious life is integral to saving the world because in and through it Christ is encountered.[8]

Aesthetics have both vision and voice. As we engage with aesthetic reality, the message of beauty responds to us in ways that encourage our awareness of God's presence and love. Experiencing an opportunity to visually see, touch, or hear something beautiful encourages the process of spiritual and emotional healing.

The immeasurable beauty of heaven is described in part in the book of Revelation. Those descriptions stimulate one's yearning for perfect beauty and the absence of sin and its many manifestations experienced in earthly life. In spiritual direction, the yearning for beauty can be acknowledged through the use of art. Not every piece of art is considered aesthetically beautiful to everyone who views, hears, or touches it, yet because art often presents subjects beyond mundane experience, it has the potential to lift one's spirit to that which is beautiful. Art may encourage the contemplation of God's holy, sublime, and matchless beauty, and of all things in heaven and on earth that reflect beauty in its many forms. Wilder views art as an expression of the beautiful:

> . . . the perceptive theologian today sees the arts not merely as servants of the church in the sense of embellishments of worship . . . . Nor is he satisfied to set the arts, as an inspirational resource, over against daily life, and to say that religion must use the sources of the Spirit—meaning Beauty, Poetry and Imagination—over against the prosaic and utilitarian world in which modern men live. . . . The theologian today recognizes that even the materialist lives not by creature comforts, prosperity and success, but by his own symbols and images, his own myths and rituals. He recognizes that the conflict today is not between matter and spirit, but between two kinds of spirit; not between prose and imagination, but between a true and false imagination; not even, finally, between

8. Mixa, "Beauty and Religious Life," lines 1–23.

ugliness and beauty, because what some would call beauty and ideality cannot save.[9]

Sublime Yet Painful Truths

"Creation is God's presence to us in beauty; the cross is God's presence to us in our brokenness and twistedness."[10] The living art forms of nature testify to both God's beauty and power. The image of the cross speaks in ways that are both beautiful and painful. In the cross one recognizes the reality of human sin and the sacrifice of God the Son to heal mankind of sin, and through faith in Christ, obtain a life of hope and promise. The cross symbolizes the suffering of God the Son, but also the beauty of redemption through the ultimate victory of the Savior: the finished work of Christ and the ultimate joyful promise of resurrection and eternal life.

An art form may be aesthetically pleasing, representing the artist's portrayal of reality or imagination, and expressing great beauty in the artist's choice of subject, style, composition, lighting, and color. However, expressing beauty in some form is not always the artist's intent. The use of art in spiritual direction often includes works that express the beautiful and joyful as well as subjects that are uncomfortable, even emotionally painful to reflect upon, as one engages with a work of art. The work may portray a subject both fearful and terrible, including physical, emotional, or spiritual struggles, which are common to human experience. The work's subject may be war, poverty, despair, grief, hopelessness, or any other range of experience and emotion related to actual historic events or arising from the artist's desire to portray various realities of life. What is beautiful lifts one's spirit and one's thoughts toward God, encouraging a desire to interact with the beauty and holiness of Deity. And yet, art that points to the hurt, struggle, and the pain of sin, loss, disappointment, and grief in human experience also has the power to lift one's spirit and thoughts to God, for to whom else can one turn when face-to-face with the difficult realities of life? The use of art in spiritual direction requires balance in presenting both the numinous and aspirational, and the eschatological realities of the faith, but also the many challenges one encounters and must deal with in daily life.

9. Wilder, "Church's New Concern with the Arts," 12–13.

10. Shea, *Stories of God*, 152.

THE CONTEXT FOR AESTHETIC UNDERSTANDING IN THE USE OF ART

Multiple layers of meaning may be evoked from interaction with artistic works. Each element of an artwork has meaning and value to the one engaging with the art. For example, one may explore a painting, considering the meaning of the subject, the artist's vision, the colorations, shapes, lighting, mood, perspective, and other characteristics.

Context affects how one perceives the aesthetic qualities of artwork. To those engaging with art in spiritual direction, the context in which a work of art is viewed is significant to the process of understanding the creator's meaning. For example, viewing a large painting or a sculptural work in a museum may elicit a very different response than would occur by viewing that same work in a book of art or an online context. Viewing a stained glass window in a great cathedral or a small church may elicit different responses in each setting, including how the viewer perceives or interprets the aesthetic qualities of the work. Reflecting on a small watercolor painted by a student and hanging in a classroom results in a response influenced by its placement in that environment. A wise director should be sensitive to the context in which directees encounter works of art, and how contextuality of setting may impact perception of meaning and aesthetic value as interpreted by the individuals engaged with art in spiritual direction.

> Discerning the presence of God in the midst of our daily lives is not always easy. However, if we discipline ourselves through the artistic acts of contemplation, perception, interpretation, and response and use them in our regular meetings with the arts, the effects of that discipline will spill over into our lives. Eventually we shall realize that every place is a sacred place, that every moment is filled with the divine Presence, and that the world is forever charged with the grandeur of God.[11]

THE CONTRAST OF ART AND ICON

In today's contemporary culture, people are inundated by visual images. The continuing advances in technology allow diverse images to appear daily as individuals use various media such as cell phones, iPads, cameras, televisions,

11. Harris in *Imaging the Word*, 13.

etc. Often the images may not represent meanings that are valuable to an individual's spiritual life and growth, but are often of a commercial nature, used to promote various vendors and the sale of their products. The use of art, not only in spiritual direction, but its use throughout the history of the church, present values that are biblically related and express, in various ways, visions that are true and eternal. Such images deserve the seer's time, including the attention of reflection and prayer, for they represent *visio* Divina: the seeing of representations and images with holy meaning and value.

As one engages with art in spiritual direction, it is important to understand and to contrast the meaning and use of traditional icons, created for religious purposes, which differ from the use of other types and styles of artistic representations. "The icon is a holy object, the form being merely a receptacle for the contents. And the content is determined by the Holy Scriptures and the Traditions of the Church. That is why the work process is marked more by discipline than by inspiration."[12] As Jeana Visel explains, "An icon usually depicts frontally a holy person confronting the viewer. In the very personal space between the person of faith and the icon, an exchange happens. One sees the image but is also *seen*."[13]

> In the Eastern tradition, an icon makes dogmatic statements in visual form. Thus the Orthodox speak of a 'language,' 'grammar' or 'semantics' of iconography. Indeed, in a strict sense, the artist does not simply paint but rather is said to 'write' an icon by using particular methods to convey particular forms that fall within an accepted canon of images. Just as the Gospel is the verbal Word of God, so the icon aims to convey the truth of Jesus.[14]

It is important, as one uses art in spiritual direction, to help directees understand the difference between iconic representative arts and all other kinds of artistic works. The use of iconic art, when the one using the art prays for the Holy Spirit's presence and guidance, can truly become life-changing as that one's knowledge and understanding of spiritual realities becomes clearer, and more attuned to the real and the true.

12. Nes, *Mystical Language of Icons*, 12.
13. Visel, *Icons in the Western Church*, 2.
14. Quenot, *Resurrection and the Icon*, 53.

ART AND PRAYER IN SPIRITUAL DIRECTION

In learning to perceive the movements of God in one's life, including the dialogue of prayer, growth in faith, obedience in thought and action, and the maturing of character, it is not uncommon that one may experience a blockage in communication with one's director when the verbal tool of discussion is used exclusively. For many, discussion alone may work well. However, the use of art has the potential to encourage a depth of discernment and understanding which discussion alone is unable to accomplish. The yearning to love God and be assured of God's own yearning for relationship with his people is a benefit of a prayerful life. In direction, one focus concerns growth in the life of prayer, which is the primary means of communication between one's spirit and the Spirit of God.

Humankind's unquenchable yearning for God, whether acknowledged and understood or not acknowledged, directs one to pursue God who is holy mystery but who is revealed through Jesus Christ. This yearning, urged by the Holy Spirit, and drawing one to prayer, is not all that encourages the believer to consistency and faithfulness in prayer. There are constant needs, including the desire for a morally good and fruitful life, and various concerns for one's family, friends, community, and the world, that serve as bidding calls by the Holy Spirit to a life where prayer is a daily constant. Art in spiritual direction is one avenue providing a stimulus through which the Holy Spirit encourages one's desire to pray. Prayer, in all its simplicity and beauty, its intense passion, hope, and love, as well as in its struggles, draws the pray-er to the disciplines of scriptural study, meditation, and contemplation. Although these disciplines do not necessarily require the use of art, engagement with art in spiritual direction has as one of its goals the development of a consistent and maturing prayer life. As one is encouraged to practice diverse kinds of prayer and other spiritual disciplines, one learns the value of waiting upon God to reveal God's self, as the Lord's presence is discerned, Spirit speaking to spirit, with silence or with words, as the pray-er waits in reverent patience.

> Prayer is a transforming activity. When you encounter God's Word, when you absorb it and open yourself to it, you risk change. Contemplation seeks deeper truth, the hope to which you are called, the justice to which the world is called, the vision of God's dominion to which all are called and which Jesus preached. Sincere contemplation, practiced over time, can change you. Make space in your life for God, for God's world, and you will find your

> relationship to that world changing as you discover connections that were overlooked before. You will find yourself engaged in God's world with your whole self—mind, heart, soul, strength.
>
> For this kind of transformation to happen, more of yourself must be revealed during prayer. Present yourself to God. Ask intimate and challenging questions of God. While in prayer, you may also discover questions about yourself—about your limitations, struggles, dreams, fears. Like Jacob . . . you may struggle intimately with God. Nothing is hidden before God. Love, forgiveness, and mercy invite you to change and to respond to God's great love.[15]

Many great works of art portray various aspects of prayer, struggles with prayer, or stimulate one's desire to enter more deeply, and with dedication, into a life of prayer. For example, Jean-Francois Millet's *L'Angélus* (also known as *The Angelus* and as *Evening Prayer*), or Vincent Van Gogh's *The Prayer*, are sublime paintings that seem to effortlessly draw one into the scenes portrayed, into the quiet, meditative nature of the compositions, forms, mood, and colors beckoning one's spirit to join in the communion of contemplation.

The Angelus, Jean-Francois Millet

15. Blain, *Imaging the World*, 13.

Stimulation of the Senses

Visual, tactile, or auditory stimulation through art can evoke or encourage prayer, memories, insights, illumination, desires, tears, and other emotional as well as intellectual responses related to one's spiritual life. Although one must understand the primacy of Scripture, and accurate understanding of Scripture as a foundation in spiritual direction, the human senses may also be used in appropriate ways to encourage understanding of God, the self, and others. Sense perception may serve as the starting point for discernment in receiving God's guidance. For example, visual images in art allow the observer to draw insights from what is portrayed, as the Holy Spirit guides their thoughts and reflections concerning such images. These insights may be valuable in the process of understanding and clarifying various emotions. Images in art may be, for example, helpful in the process of dealing with grief, fear, life transitions, or buried emotions, for art often evokes personal memories. As one approaches art prayerfully, the Holy Spirit will guide the engager to discover the meaning and value of the message conveyed by the art. Again, all engagement with artistic works should be tested by comparing one's insights from the process with the veracity of Scripture.

A sensitive spiritual director will understand when and when not to use various art forms in the process of direction. It is important not to overwhelm directees with visual, auditory, or tactile stimulation through the use of many works of art, but carefully assist each person to discover which art forms and individual works are personally meaningful. The use of art cannot be forced; one should be enthusiastic about engaging with an artwork before the process will be of value to spiritual direction. When the type of art and specific example are chosen, then it is helpful to stay with that image for a reasonable time, companioning the one directed as he or she explores the various meanings derived from the work.

One of the values in the use or art is that the process often uncovers spiritual and/or emotional needs that require further processing in the proper context to result in the directee's continuing progress in spiritual, emotional, and relational healing.

Engagement with a work of art, when guided by the Holy Spirit, may give rise to interpretations of the work's possible meanings to an individual or group. The Spirit may give discernment relative to a work of art providing insights and allowing the work of art to serve as a starting place for gaining new knowledge, insights, and wisdom. In engagement with art. as individuals or groups are sensitive to the presence and leadings of the Holy Spirit, the process of prayerful reflection encourages spiritual, emotional, and relational growth and wholeness.

The Disabled: Exploring Art in Spiritual Direction

The disabled are not limited in exploring layers of meaning in various artistic works. The quality of visuality is not limited to the sighted. A person with visual disablement, who was previously sighted, may have the capacity to "see" paintings through mental images as an artistic work is described to them. Also, sculptures may be explored through touch, and music enjoyed through the sense of hearing. For those individuals who are sighted, but do not "see" mental images when thinking, praying, or reading, art allows a new and needed dimension to their visual ability and therefore enhances the practices of prayer, reflection, and scriptural meditation, thus increasing their discernment of the Spirit's movements in their lives.

Engagement with visual forms of art evokes various levels of emotional response. For example, if an individual is struggling with a troubling or repressed emotion, engagement with a work of art may serve to uncover emotions, allowing them to emerge into consciousness, where they may be acknowledged and prayerfully examined. Discussing those emotions with one's director assists in gaining greater self-knowledge and moving toward inner healing of spiritual needs. The primary goal for the use of art in spiritual direction is, of course, spiritual growth, not healing of the memories or emotions. However, one cannot separate emotional, physical, or spiritual healing from the process of spiritual growth. Therefore, engagement with art in spiritual direction, and working through the process of reflecting on artwork to gain spiritual insights, will always benefit one's needs for healing and wholeness.

New Technologies and Spiritual Direction

In a highly technologically advanced era, where people are constantly barraged with countless visual images and auditory receptions through media, individuals are not always aware that overexposure to sensual stimulation may limit or dull the value of using art in spiritual direction. This limitation is due to the fact that spiritual direction requires time and understanding to comprehend the deeper meanings received through the process. Sensory overload may dull one's ability to appreciate the rich potential of various art forms in one's spiritual life. A painting, sculpture, photograph, textile art, or musical work requires an attitude of openness and patience to interact meaningfully with the art form. Patience, engagement in the reflective process, including prayer, are needed to unlock those secrets the art may reveal, or emotions the art piece may evoke, which open an individual to the divine mystery of God, and the unfolding revelation of God's presence in one's life.

Despite the inherent dangers of an exponentially advancing technological age, spiritual directors must navigate the new contemporary terrain of these advancements. For example, they need to consider the fact that technology affects the ways people receive and process information in innovation age. Directors can increase their effectiveness in this current age of communication advances by considering if and how technological changes may affect the internal movements of the spiritual self as well as outward actions motivated by one's spirituality.

> In addition to the theological grounding for the importance of the image . . . there is another important reason to pay attention to the visual arts. The contemporary generation has been raised and nourished by images; it has an inescapably visual imagination. Regardless of whether one considers this good or bad, for this generation, aesthetics counts more than epistemology. Actually, this is the theme that has deep roots in the Christian tradition. As St. Augustine put it, what you enjoy (love!) is more important than what you know! Critiquing contemporary culture has been a favorite pastime for Christians since the Reformation.[16]

Contemporary developments and changes in the ways people perceive reality and communicate inform the various models and traditions in the ministry of spiritual direction. Historically, it is difficult to find evidence supporting the use of art in any formal and substantive ways in spiritual direction. Certain Christian groups developed during the Reformation, for example the Anabaptist tradition, eschewed many forms of artistic expression. However, those churches remaining in the liturgical-sacramental tradition have continued to embrace diverse forms of art as accepted and valuable assets in the life of the church.

16. Dyrness, *Visual Faith*, 20.

A Stained Glass Vision of Truth

During my first ministry position, I met an elderly woman with a strong, vibrant personality. She spoke frankly about her spiritual struggles throughout life. She loved the local church where she and her parents worshiped, where she had been baptized, nurtured in the faith, and continued to attend services well into her elder years. She explained to me that several pastors had served the congregation throughout the years of her membership, each with their own particular style of preaching, teaching, and pastoral leadership. She indicated that changing pastors did not bother her in the least for she could always experience the spiritual constancy of the sanctuary's architectural and artistic beauty. My friend explained that as she sat in her pew on Sunday mornings, she raised her vision upward to the massive and stunning stained glass windows in the sanctuary. The magnificent windows extended the full width of the chancel, behind the altar, and depicted in countless colored mosaic pieces, brilliantly arranged, a visual gospel expressing events in the life of Jesus Christ. This faithful believer declared that every Sunday she "saw" a new sermon in the expansive panorama of the widows, and she "heard" the message presented by the artist's depiction of truth as she worshiped. No matter how often leadership might change, her encounter with this stained glass vision of truth would continue to draw her wordlessly, but powerfully, to her Savior and Lord.

"The Painted Church"

A well-known and stunning example of *visio divina* (sacred seeing), a contemplative practice in which the pray-er seeks the presence and guidance of the Lord as he or she initially focuses on a particular image, is the congregational home of what is often called "St. Benedict's Painted Church," located at Honaunau, on the Big Island of Hawaii, which sits above Kealakekua Bay:

> An unassuming white building with a sloped green roof the wooden exterior of St. Benedict's Catholic Church gives nothing away about the beauty of its interior. As you walk the creaky floorboards of this 19th century church you are surrounded by vivid frescos depicting various stories from the Bible.
>
> The Belgian priest Father John Velghe used these six frescos to teach the spiritual lessons to native Hawaiians who could not read. Behind the altar, the talented, yet untrained, Father Velghe created a rendering of the nave of a Spanish Gothic Cathedral. The

arches and columns continue on far past the physical walls of the church. The church still holds regular masses during the week and on weekends.[17]

St. Benedict's Catholic Church, Honaunau, Hawaii

St. Benedict's images were not painted by Father Velghe as representing depictions from his own imagination, but are images by which the priest attempted to truthfully portray visual impressions of various events contained in the New Testament. The paintings affirm the priest's love for God's people, whom he was sent to shepherd. They also attest to a visual miracle: a gift of artistic beauty and truth of expression given by God to Father Velghe, so the Lord's people would be blessed by the reality of Holy Scripture, represented in visual form.

Visuality as Part of Work and Worship

Just as art has enriched the life and worship of the church throughout the centuries, spiritual direction is enriched and saved from a one-dimensional approach, becoming more sensitive to the needs of those directed when the ministry is open to engagement with various forms of artistic expression. Visual sense, in particular, is important to the process by which one relates to God, to others, and to the world. Visuality is part of work and of worship, and therefore essential to the ministry of spiritual direction. For the director to simply present the question "what are you *seeing* in everyday

17. Derrick, "Painted Church," lines 1–2; 4–9.

life that speaks to your relationship with God?" can begin a profoundly important conversation which may flow into engagement with various art forms. Asking the right questions stimulates exploration of the ways interaction with art reveals truth to an individual about his or her life and faith development.

Ultimately, using art for the purpose of seeking the Holy Spirit's presence and guidance is meant to draw the person engaging with the art to a place of greater desire for loving and serving God. The use of art in spiritual direction is meant to reveal Scriptural truth so that one will pursue the biblical value of living a holy life, one fully given for the purposes of God.

PART III

Practical Applications for Using Art in Spiritual Direction

Chapter 5

Supporting Christian Formation through the Use of Art

"We can only learn to know ourselves and do what we can—namely, surrender our will and fulfill God's will in us."

—St. Teresa of Avila (1515–82)

IMITATIO CHRISTI

Formative spirituality, the formation, conformation, and transformation of one's life to *imitatio Christi,* encompasses the whole of one's life and faith development. Spiritual development and maturation are based on Trinitarian reality. The realities of God as revealed (the kataphatic life) and God as concealed (the apophatic life—the mystery of God) comprise dimensions of one's continuing journey in Christian spirituality. Artistic expressions may serve as catalysts to encourage and support directees' spiritual growth and maturation in all aspects and experiences of life and faith.

At its foundation, spiritual direction is primarily about one's growth and maturation in relationship with God and with others. As one grows in relationship with God, one's manner of relating to others changes in various ways. Therefore, the use of art, which has power to reveal truths concerning relationships with God and others, is important to the process of spiritual formation, conformation, and transformation in Christ.

A Mature Disciple

An important goal of spiritual formation is maturing as a disciple of Jesus Christ. The maturing disciple of Christ becomes more discerning and truth-based relative to one's feelings, attitudes, and practices involving relationships with God and with others. Growth in Christ, including the ability to love others, will include becoming more sensitive in hearing and responding to the promptings of the Holy Spirit as one interacts with others. Maturing in one's life of prayer, which encompasses a primary means of communication with God, includes concomitant growth in the ability to respond based on knowledge, understanding, sensitivity, and love in relationships with God and others. George Tooker's painting, *Girl Praying*, sensitively expresses the inward beauty, outwardly and silently manifested, in the holy communication of a young believer.

Girl Praying, George Claire Tooker

The ministry of spiritual direction is not limited or compartmentalized to encouraging spiritual growth only in one's devotional life. Spiritual direction includes the purpose of developing maturity in Christlike character including humility, the ability to forgive, and the motivation to unselfishly love others. Spiritual growth in one's life of prayer, worship, and discernment in hearing and responding to the still, small voice of the Holy Spirit, will influence one's actions in thinking, planning, and living truthfully in the authentic faith that has been revealed to the church through the incarnational life of Jesus Christ.

One's relationships with others has the potential to either encourage spiritual growth or limit that growth, depending on one's sensitivity to hearing and obeying the Holy Spirit in all personal interactions with others. When spiritual direction results in learning to discern the voice and the movements of God in one's life, then this maturation process results in the ability to relate gracefully and with integrity to all others.

Art and Relationships

The fact that countless works of art focus on relationships as their subject or theme, points to the richness of art as a resource for spiritual growth in learning to interact graciously with others, and showing honor, forgiveness, and love for those persons who are part of one's life. For example, Dutch artist Rembrandt van Rijn's moving portrayal in oil on canvas titled *The Return of the Prodigal Son*[1] presents an opportunity for reflection on one's relationships, both with the heavenly Father and with one's earthly father: how these relationships influence one's spirituality, character, overall perception of life, and the process of spiritual and emotional growth, including healing and reconciliation.

1. The classic painting is Rembrandt's expression of Jesus' parable from Luke 15:11–32. The parable expresses the heavenly Father's love and forgiveness as represented in the story by an earthly father, and how these qualities are perceived and responded to by the father's two sons: a faithful son and a rebellious son who repents and returns to his father.

The Return of the Prodigal Son, Rembrandt van Rijn

The affective life, with its broad and deep range of human emotions, cannot be separated from the overall equation of spiritual growth and wholeness of the human person. In the Hebrew language the human person is understood as whole. Body, soul, and spirit are viewed as integrated and cannot be compartmentalized and dealt with individually, apart from each one's integration with the other two. Therefore, the intellect, the will, and the emotions are not simply separate aspects of the human person, each one operating independently of the others. In addressing what may appear as a wholly emotional issue, the director must realize that each person brings all of himself or herself into the equation of dealing with any specific aspect of life and spirituality. The director must realize that the use of art not only engages the senses but engages the totality of the individual.

Being and Becoming in Christ

The New Testament's view of spiritual formation does not categorize one's spirituality as a single aspect of life but instead indicates that spiritual growth, the focus of one's life upon becoming a disciple of Christ, is all that one needs to fully realize God's purposes for every aspect, every nuance, of life. Being and becoming in Christ, as a disciple follows the teachings of Jesus Christ and is empowered by the Holy Spirit, will encompass every aspect of one's life in an integrated way. For example, the devotional disciplines connected to formation, including worship, prayer, study, meditation of Scripture, and other practices, provide the focus one needs for continuing growth and maturity as a disciple of Jesus Christ. It is within the context of one's daily devotion to God that one develops and matures in character, in understanding, in wisdom of God's ways, and in the motivation of obedience: following God's will in one's life. The practice of each discipline engages, in diverse ways, the physical self, the affective itself, the intellect, the will, the spirit, memories, and relationships. However, it is not practice of the disciplines that is responsible for transformation through the renewing of the mind, but rather it is the loving power of God's presence as one lives obediently in daily relationship with Christ, guided by the Holy Spirit, doing all that is needed to live faithfully as Jesus' disciple.

The Journey of Spiritual Formation

The journey of spiritual formation includes the process of conformation: conforming one's thoughts, desires, intentions, and actions to the revealed will of God in Jesus Christ, as understood from Scripture. This growth away from self-seeking desires and inclinations toward God's will occurs over time, involving the movements of the Holy Spirit in guiding the individual to understand the difference between making choices that are detrimental to one's faith and life, as opposed to making choices that are beneficial to one's overall spiritual growth. As one understands these differences, the Spirit provides empowerment to make wise choices relative to one's faith and life. This molding of volitional integrity requires a growing trust in God and God's purposes for the individual. Maturing in volitional integrity requires changing an individual's desires from selfish to selfless, from self-centeredness to other-centeredness, and from self-focus to an outward focus of one's thoughts and actions. This movement from selfishness toward selflessness indicates a willing discipleship in following the teachings of Jesus Christ. There is necessarily conflict in this process as a relationship grows in love and spiritual intimacy with the Lord. The conflict arises because one's self-centeredness and selfishness are threatened. This perceived threat is interpreted as requiring a loss of identity and autonomy, rather than the process of emerging as one's true self as personal identity and wholeness become centered in and identified with Jesus Christ. In reality, submission to the revealed will of God represents receiving a gift of authentic freedom as an individual matures in the ability to choose what is holy in motivation and intention. Such decisions are not possible when one remains dependent upon the self, rather than seeking the guidance of the Holy Spirit, in choosing spiritual resources and in making decisions.

Spiritual awareness must include knowledge of any resistance or reluctance in receiving and following the teachings of Jesus. Living a life of faith requires the process of forgoing the human inclination to trust the self more than God, inwardly assured that God, above all others, can be trusted in every situation and in meeting every human need. Human reasoning is limited, and yet we often cling to it, whereas trust in God requires letting go of control and surrendering one's life to Christ: a necessity for spiritual joy and maturation. The process is challenging because the self desires to control life and fears surrender. However, through the indwelling Spirit, one is empowered to begin the spiritual journey of learning to trust. One may tend to deny the movements of the Holy Spirit, or simply turn away from the Spirit's guidance. The proclivity to seek the self above seeking God results in turning away from God to obey the fallacies of self-understanding or the counsel of others who are unable to discern, or refuse to heed, the leading of the Spirit.

The ministry of spiritual direction supplies a level of spiritual accountability in one's life journey of spiritual formation. The director's responsibility is to provide objectivity in the direction process, as he or she discerns an individual's spiritual needs. From this objective stance, the director may often detect various levels of mistrust or abnormal fear of God, selfishness, or other hindrances to an individual's spiritual growth. The ministry of spiritual direction intends to assist the directee in understanding the edges of experience, expectations, temptations, and desires, where spiritual dangers lurk in his or her personality or actions. Rather than naming these challenges, the wise director guides an individual to recognize and openly acknowledge these areas of spiritual and volitional immaturity.

The director provides comfort, companionship, community, guidance, and a sense of safety and security to accompany and encourage a directee in facing difficult spiritual truths concerning life and faith. A director is the "*anam cara*" or soul friend[2] to the one who has come for spiritual direction. Jesus promised: "For where two or three have gathered together in My name, I am there in their midst."[3] When believers gather together, the presence of the Holy Spirit infuses their relationship with a desire to share the realities and power of their faith and the pathways of their spiritual journeys with one another. It is a daunting prospect to share the raw material of one's spiritual concerns with another person, no matter how trusted the person. It is just as daunting a prospect to know God is listening and to discern the Lord's guidance. The spiritual director provides support and comfort to the seeking soul while lovingly but firmly urging one forward as they mature in the knowledge and experience of living as Christ's disciple. The director must help an individual maintain balance between experiencing a necessary degree of comfort in their spiritual journey and yet taking the risk to move forward in acknowledging truth, and practicing spiritual disciplines for the purpose of growth in character. As one must learn in maturing spiritually, Christian formation is not a process that always brings comfort, but ultimately the process results in joy as one matures in love for God and for others.

One blunt and pithy example of an opinion concerning the importance of spiritual direction is attributed to St. Brigid of Ireland who alledgedly opined, in a typically humorous Irish manner, that a person without a soul friend compares to a body without a head.[4] No doubt Brigid understood

2. In the Gaelic language "*anam*" is defined as soul; "*cara*" means friend. *Anam Cara: A Book of Celtic Wisdom* by John O'Donahue discusses the meaning of "anam cara" as understood and practiced in the Celtic Christian tradition of spiritual direction.

3. Matt 18:20.

4. "About the year 470 she founded a double monastery at Cill-Dara (Kildare) and was abbess of the convent, the first in Ireland. The foundation developed into a center of learning and spirituality, and around it grew up the Cathedral city of Kildare." "St. Brigid

that Christianity is not a faith of solitariness, although silence and solitude are necessary for the spiritual life, but consists of balancing the disciplines of community and solitude. The adage that one cannot be a Christian alone is certainly true. The solitary Christian who avoids accountability and community is more vulnerable to temptation, delusion, and other evils. The essence of spiritual formation is growth in understanding and spiritual intimacy with the Lord; moving away from the false securities of human life to engage fully in glorifying God and blessing the lives of others. The ministry of spiritual direction is meant to support the process of maturing in Christ, including the desire and effort to live a truly meaningful life, one that is not self-centered or arrogant with spiritual pride, but humbly open and giving to others.

In the process of spiritual formation, the use of art can speak in countless ways, encouraging the Christian disciple to rise above his or her own self-centeredness, moving to a new vision, one focused upon loving and serving God and others. The Holy Spirit's teaching is available and powerful through the mediated communication of art to shake the foundations of self-centeredness, pride, and spiritual apathy. Engagement with art, properly applied, can clearly reveal one's suffering, desires, needs, and the nature of our struggle to know God.

The Use of Art as a Spiritual Discipline

To use art in spiritual direction provides an opportunity to practice a discipline with the potential to support and encourage one's focus upon God, through the medium of artistic expression. It is not that the discipline of using art in and of itself matures one or makes one holy; only God can form and change the individual. However, a spiritual discipline allows the individual to give one's time and attention to God. It is in the presence of God that one is formed, conformed, and transformed to become wholly devoted to God. Art, if used wisely in spiritual direction, will have benefits that relate to the totality of a person's life. Attempting to categorize art in spiritual direction as a compartmentalized practice is to miss an opportunity to companion the one directed in exploring how engagement with art touches all of one's life.

of Ireland," lines 9–11.

Formation, Conformation, and Transformation

Biblically and historically, there are diversities in approaches and models of spiritual formation. Formation in Christ, growth in conformation to the will of God through the power of the Holy Spirit, and transformation through the progressive renewal of the mind, are the concerns of formative spirituality. Although these three areas define the processes and outcomes of spiritual growth and maturity, one cannot overlook the unique ways in which God interacts with individuals and communities in the process of growth in Christ.

In considering the Old and New Testament examples that point specifically to an individual's spiritual formation, it is important for the spiritual director to consider the wealth of artistic works that express an aspect or aspects of Christian formative spirituality. A spiritual director, in using art, can pose the question to the directee as to his or her perception of how the artwork relates to their spiritual formation and, in particular, how the themes and portrayals in the artwork relate specifically to his or her own Christian growth and maturity.

The Law as Formative

The Old Testament details the importance of the law in the spiritual forming and continuing lives of God's people. The Bible is replete with the history of how the Lord's commandments and the faith community's successes and failures as they attempted to live within the boundaries of these commands, shaped the spiritual history of God's people. Their knowledge of the law and attempts to obey the Lord's statutes were constant and formative aspects of the lived theology of God's ancient people. Knowledge of the law gave the community a sense of shared identity, a sense of purpose, and an understanding of their own limitations and sinfulness in their attempts to obey God's laws.

Acknowledging the Realities of Life and Faith

The New Testament provides numerous examples of Jesus' interaction with individuals and groups throughout his ministries of teaching, preaching, healing, and deliverance. Both his formal and informal exchanges with others influenced their ideas, actions, and understanding of life and faith as individuals and groups encountered the Messiah. The Gospels' accounts convey Jesus' discernment of people's needs: their hopes, fears, struggles, and their need to understand and embrace a relationship with God. The ministry of spiritual direction must be attuned to these same realities of an individual's needs concerning life and faith. It must provide a loving approach and yet the willingness to ask, to question, and to encourage an individual to share what may be previously unexpressed, including deeply held emotions related to essential needs, desires, hopes, plans, and questions.

One example of Jesus' sensitive, loving approach in healing is his ministry to Peter, who was devastated by the reality of his sin in denying Jesus three times in those dark hours preceding the Lord's passion. Following Jesus' resurrection, as the Lord reunited with his disciples, he gently, yet firmly, led the disciple through a process that allowed Peter the opportunity to honestly confess the nature and quality of his love for Jesus. Peter had miserably failed in his love for his Lord by committing a stark betrayal. In John's Gospel, Jesus helps Peter confess his new understanding, in precise terms, of the quality of his love for Jesus. No more is Peter the spontaneous braggart who overestimates his love for and faithfulness to Jesus. Peter's betrayal has awakened him to the depth of his own faults and sin. As John's Gospel account shares, in the following passage, Jesus lovingly heals and restores Peter's relationship with him in a way that signals a new beginning to Peter's life and his subsequent faithful commitment to Jesus:

> So when they had finished breakfast, Jesus said to Simon Peter, 'Simon, son of John, do you love Me more than these?' He said to Him, 'Yes, Lord; You know that I love You' He said to him, 'Tend My lambs' He said to him again a second time, 'Simon, son of John, do you love Me?'He said to Him, 'Yes, Lord; You know that I love You' He said to him, 'Shepherd My sheep.' He said to him the third time, 'Simon, son of John, do you love Me?' Peter was grieved because He said to him the third time, 'Do you love Me?' And he said to Him, 'Lord, You know all things; You know that I love You' Jesus said to him, 'Tend My sheep'[5]

This sensitive but powerful interchange between Jesus and Peter informs the very nature of spiritual direction and how a discerning, sensitive approach to a person's inner needs defines the ways in which spiritual direction impacts the Christian formation, conformation, and transformation of an individual life. As an example of how art may be valuable in the process of

5. John21:15–17 NASB.

Christian catechesis and development, the moving and powerful painting *Tears of St. Peter* by Doménikos Theotokópoulos (known as El Greco), provides a focal point for director and directee to explore Peter's journey of formative spirituality from betrayal to restoration by Jesus and how this may relate to the directee's own spiritual formation.[6]

The Tears of St. Peter, El Greco

6. This painting was completed c. 1587–96 and is housed in the Museo Soumaya, Mexico City, Mexico.

The Pauline Letters: Formed in Prayer

The New Testament epistles continue the thread of formative spirituality in recounting many events expressing how the apostles and other individuals and groups were formed in faith, often experiencing miraculous growth and change in their lives as they embraced and began living the gospel's truth.

The apostle Paul tenderly expressed his heart to the church at Galatia: "My children, with whom I am again in labor until Christ is formed in you. . . ."[7] Reflecting on the meaning of the term "formed" in English, one may envision the idea of creating an internal reality, of making or molding something to become what it is meant to be as a completed whole. It is interesting that Paul recognizes the progressive nature of formation as he expresses his own spiritual labor and practical ministry in desiring that the reality of Christ will dwell individually and collectively in the lives of the Galatian believers.

To the church at Ephesus Paul eloquently and passionately intercedes for God's people presenting a Trinitarian theology of spiritual formation:

> For this reason I too, having heard of the faith in the Lord Jesus which exists among you and your love for all the saints, I do not cease giving thanks for you, while making mention of you in my prayers; that the God of our Lord Jesus Christ, the Father of glory, may give to you a spirit of wisdom and of revelation in the knowledge of Him. I pray that the eyes of your heart may be enlightened, so that you will know what is the hope of His calling, what are the riches of the glory of His inheritance in the saints, and what is the surpassing greatness of His power toward us who believe. These are in accordance with the working of the strength of His might which He brought about in Christ, when He raised Him from the dead and seated Him at His right hand in the heavenly places, far above all rule and authority and power and dominion, and every name that is named, not only in this age but also in the one to come. And He put all things in subjection under His feet, and gave Him as head over all things to the church which is His body, the fullness of Him who fills all in all.[8]

From this passage, we understand the authority, the movements, and the commitment of God in forming a faithful disciple of Christ. God is the

7. Gal 4:19 NASB..
8. Eph1:15–23 NASB.

initiator, he who acts, he who gives wisdom and revelation, who enlightens the heart and empowers one's life with the knowledge of God's reality as active and powerful, allowing one to live by faith. Paul continues to focus on the importance of spiritual formation in his letter to Ephesian believers:

> Therefore I ask you not to lose heart at my tribulations on your behalf, for they are your glory. For this reason I bow my knees before the Father, from whom every family in heaven and on earth derives its name, that He would grant you, according to the riches of His glory, to be strengthened with power through His Spirit in the inner man, so that Christ may dwell in your hearts through faith; and that you, being rooted and grounded in love, may be able to comprehend with all the saints what is the breadth and length and height and depth, and to know the love of Christ which surpasses knowledge, that you may be filled up to all the fullness of God.[9]

God-initiated Spiritual Formation

Paul's prayer in this context emphasizes the interior formation of faith through the movements of God in one's life. Paul indicates the changes resulting from this formation and the ultimate goals of these formative movements of God in the life of the believer. The passage expresses not only the reality of God-initiated formative spirituality, but also the conformation and transformation of the believer in Christ, and the beauty of this process. Ephesians 1 and 3 stunningly reveal the reality and necessity of spiritual formation. They affirm the Trinitarian nature of spiritual formation, the healing of the inner self, and the wholeness resulting from the processes of spiritual formation, conformation, and transformation in Christ as one matures throughout life, becoming more and more "filled up to all the fullness of God."[10] "The saving merits and energizing life of Christ now come to us through the Holy Spirit, who is present with us in the world. Presently the Spirit is our point of contact with—indeed, our lifeline to—the triune God."[11]

9. Eph 3:14–19 NASB.

10. Eph 3:19 NASB..

11. Scorgie, *Little Guide to Christian Spirituality*, 26.

Why Spiritual Direction is Important to Formation in Christ

The realities of formation expressed in Paul's letter to the nascent church at Ephesus are relative to spiritual direction, for both Christian formation and spiritual direction have in common the goals expressed by the apostle. The ministry of spiritual direction has the goal of maturing one's character to reflect thoughts and actions that are Christlike. The goal of *imitatio Christi* is common to both formative spirituality and spiritual direction. Therefore, spiritual direction, as a discipline and also as a ministry, constitutes a practice supportive of an individual's spiritual formation. Art, as explored in the ministry of spiritual direction, becomes a resource to encourage one's movements toward greater intimacy with God, accurate knowledge of the self and one's needs, and how these needs are met in one's maturing relationship with God.

Structures for Accountability

Direction allows for structures of accountability, for opportunities to share one's thoughts, needs, desires, and dreams concerning life with God, in a context where "practicing the presence of God"[12] teaches an individual to discern the voice and movements of the Holy Spirit in one's life. Formation requires an understanding of the spiritual realities concerning one's relationships. Spiritual formation requires one's continuing relationship with God as well as a concomitant relationship with community. It is not possible to mature in Christ without participation in both contexts for spiritual growth. Drawing away from others in solitude and silence, to pray, worship, study, and mediate on Scripture, to contemplate the wonder and goodness of God, is essential to a spiritual life which has the potential for change and growth. In the context of community where quiet contemplative practices seek the balance of interaction with others, one faces the need to mature in the ability to unconditionally love others, to grow in the ability to forgive, to trust, and to evidence a gracious understanding of one's brothers and sisters in Christ. Community allows us to come face-to-face with the truth about our relationships with others: our faults, sins, and emotional limitations in living peacefully and in unity with one's faith community. Through

12. The phrase "practicing the presence of God" is taken from the collected writings, as compiled by Fr. Joseph de Beaufort, of seventeenth century Carmelite monk Brother Lawrence, and published by the title *Brother Lawrence*..

interactions with a body of believers, we recognize and define our needs for mercy, care, and accountability, as well as experiencing the joys of affirmation, encouragement, support, and the corporate necessity of worshiping and ministering together in Christ. Spiritual direction is a ministry that guides us away from an insular existence; the tendency to isolate oneself in times of struggle, in other difficult seasons in life, or at times when we fear our innermost frailties becoming exposed to others.

Art as a Resource to Support Understanding and Growth

Art, which may be used in one's private times of prayer and worship, as well as in those times of corporate sharing and interactive prayer and worship, provides an additional resource in the journey to becoming formed in Christ. By using various art forms in spiritual direction, one may experience a depth of understanding and growth in spiritual maturity that may not result to the same degree without engagement with art forms. The employment of the physical senses is important to formation. These abilities are among the gifts of humanness, to be used in prayer, worship, engagement with art, and other spiritual disciplines, for the glory of God.

Spiritual Formation in the Context of God Revealed and God as Mystery

How does spiritual formation relate to both the kataphatic and apophatic aspects of Christian spirituality? As previously discussed, the term "kataphatic" refers to God-revealed. The term "apophatic" refers to God who is hidden, or the mystery of God. Both words derive from the ancient Greek language. The formative spirituality of both the individual and the community includes experiencing the presence and movements of God in both dimensions. The two dimensions, when understood, allow a balanced understanding of one's relationship with God. One moves toward understanding the reality of God, who chooses to reveal himself in Jesus Christ. Yet in many times and ways, God seems to withdraw, mysterious and hidden at times from our experience.

Those who have faith in Jesus Christ live with this dynamic tension between the God who reveals God's self and the God who is holy mystery. Primarily, God has revealed God's self in Jesus Christ:

> God, after He spoke long ago to the fathers in the prophets in many portions and in many ways, in these last days has spoken to us in His Son, whom He appointed heir of all things, through whom also He made the world. And He is the radiance of His glory and the exact representation of His nature, and upholds all things by the word of His power.[13]

Jesus spoke to Philip about the revelation of the Father in him: "Jesus said to him, Have I been so long with you, and yet you have not come to know Me, Philip? He who has seen Me has seen the Father; how can you say, 'Show us the Father?'"[14] In contrast, the prophet Isaiah spoke of God as profound eternal mystery: "Truly, You are a God who hides Himself, O God of Israel, Savior!"[15] God is knowable to the extent he allows, yet mysterious also the extent he chooses, for his divine purposes. Just as our intellectual knowledge of God is always limited, so also is our lived theology: the daily understanding and experience of our relationship with God. The process involving the unfolding knowledge of, and relationship with the Holy Trinity, is eternal in all its aspects. Yet, the full reality of God is unknowable to the human mind and experience. The One who is omniscient, omnipresent, and omnipotent cannot be fully known by the Lord's creatures; by those with human limitations. Humankind lives in the earthly context of three dimensions, and therefore our interaction with God is mediated communication. Through prayer, worship, and other spiritual practices, we communicate with God, and God communicates with us through the mediation of the Holy Spirit.

In the process of spiritual formation we find this tension: the greater knowledge of God, the face-to-face presence with Jesus Christ which we desire, will only be revealed when we exist in the dimension of eternity. The tension between living life on earth is a journey of both joy and sadness, and yet during that journey, moving upward in faith toward one's eternal destiny, is poignantly portrayed in Ellis Wilson's painting *The Funeral Procession*. We live with an often urgent longing to part the veil of God's hiddenness, to know and to see those eternal realities that now we dimly imagine, but will someday be fully revealed to us as we are in the near and glorious presence of God. For now, in this earthly life, we are called to the disciplines of patience, contentment, and full surrender to God's purposes.

13. Heb 1: 1–3 NASB.
14. John 4:19 NASB.
15. Isa 45:15 NASB.

The tension between what is, and what will be, is a necessary tension. As we embrace and accept that tension, we grow in faith. Our faith requires that we trust in God who is beyond our experience of this world. It is through the virtue of trust that we grow in relationship with God and with others, maturing in love, which requires us to reach beyond those things known to us through the reality of three dimensions.

The Funeral Procession, Ellis Wilson

No matter the degree of knowledge we possess about those whom we love, even those most intimate to our lives, there is much about them that remains hidden from our knowledge. In the unfolding of life we seek to know more, to understand more, and to enter more deeply into the life of God and into the life of those closest to us. We desire to grow in grace, knowledge, understanding, and wisdom, through the unfolding process of God's movements in our lives and our responses to those movements.

As one matures in the ability to overcome anxiety, to remain patient and at peace, one learns to live gracefully with the reality of both the revealed and the hidden aspects of life with God and with others. In spiritual direction we may begin to see this reality of dynamic tension more clearly, and learn its meaning as well as its necessity. This tension actually assists growth in the ability to engender trust in the character and the promises of God. In learning to trust God, a primary process in spiritual formation, it is necessary to let go of one's dependence on intellectual and affective assurances of God's presence, learning to rely upon God during those times when hearing the Lord's voice inwardly, or discerning the Lord's presence, are not perceived. There are times when cognizance of the Holy Spirit's guidance seems absent from one's life. Living with the mystery of God is one of the tensions believers face in any season of life. One must learn to depend on the truth of God, as revealed in Holy Scripture, and make decisions and choose actions according to the perfection and unmistakable infallibility of the Lord's written word.

In a work of art there are both revealed and hidden aspects in the artist's expression. A painting cannot convey the full reality and meaning of a particular theme, scene, person, or object. In a musical work, at some point the notes come to an end, and it is left to the hearer's imagination to reflect on how the music, if continued, would sound. Sculpture is limited in what it reveals. Often a sculpted figure is experienced in a museum, a courtyard, or in other outdoor spaces that are not contextual to the sculpture's subject. We may imagine, based on the information we know about the figure or object portrayed in the sculpture, what the actual context of the sculpture might be in real life. In textile art there is a beginning and end to the work—the materials start and they stop at certain points—therefore the flow of the work is finite, providing the viewer a limited revelation of what truths the textile might further reveal or represent if the art piece were endless. In the Orthodox tradition, the icon is created to draw the viewer to the reality of God above and beyond what is seen in the symbolic representations within the icon. The use of art in spiritual direction is also iconic in that works of art are for the purpose of calling the beholder to discern the greater reality; that which is beyond what is revealed to mind and eyes, therefore encouraging the viewer to become courageously open to exploring the holy and wholly other who is God.

Models of Formation and Diversities in Perspective

In post-biblical history, as the Christian faith spread throughout the known world across the time span of many centuries, the diversity in denominations, groups, and movements gave rise to various emerging approaches and models of spiritual formation. The similarities in various formation models are evident in that the primary goal of Christian formation is maturation in Christlikeness, becoming more like Jesus in character and in expressed actions.

Christian faith traditions include numerous approaches or models, many similar, and yet each one inclusive of distinct ways to address the necessity of growth and maturity in faith and practice. Approaches or models of spiritual formation are contextualized; they have differed and changed throughout the centuries depending on the theology and practices of each denomination or group. Although each model of formation has commonalities with others, each one is distinct in its history, variances in theology, methods of catechesis, and the understanding of discipleship and sacramental life. Overall, differing models of spiritual formation, although orthodox as to the basics of Christian worldview and theology, vary in certain aspects of how one is to express Christian life and faith. These differences are due to many factors including, but not limited to, the dissemination and availability of Scripture, movements of revival and renewal, changes in leadership, events in secular history, the uses of contemporary technology that have bearing on the Christian community, and other factors.

It is important for spiritual directors to possess knowledge concerning a directee's faith tradition, including that tradition's theology and approach to formative spirituality. A director must not take for granted that he or she knows the approach or model of spiritual formation the directee has been accustomed to in his or her denomination. The directee may have recently affiliated with or become a member of a specific denomination or group, having experienced his or her earlier formative spirituality in a different Christian tradition. Or perhaps the directee is a "cradle" member of the denomination or group, and has been spiritually molded by the group's particular approach to Christian formation. One of the director's tasks during the initial meeting with individuals new to spiritual direction is to encourage them to reflect upon and share both their previous and current experiences in formative spirituality. This information is essential, helping the director understand the directee's spiritual journey. As directors research the model of spiritual formation common to a directee's particular denomination or group, the information gained from this research will assist in determining how to best introduce and integrate the use of art into the individual's process of spiritual direction.

Directors may not be well-informed concerning the history of a directee's tradition, including its history, theology, and approach to spiritual formation. If a spiritual director is not knowledgeable concerning a directee's experience of spiritual formation, there exists a certain level of inability for each one to communicate with the other. If a directee is not knowledgeable concerning the model of spiritual formation in his or her tradition, the director who has taken time to study the directee's tradition has the ability to share their knowledge with the directee. A well-prepared director can greatly benefit a directee by helping the individual understand how one's tradition or denomination relates to his or her spiritual journey and how this journey relates to every aspect of one's life.

It may be that the directee was born into a certain denomination or group, and at some point changed to another Christian faith tradition. It is also possible that a directee has experienced spiritual life in various communities representing several Christian or other faith traditions. The director must provide an opportunity to discuss how interaction with these various denominations, groups, or interaction with non-Christian traditions, has influenced the directee's spiritual growth process or changed the directee's ideas and practices concerning their faith. The director must not overlook the fact that each individual brings to the ministry of spiritual direction his or her own spiritual history. A director needs to acknowledge, honor, and assist each individual to explore and to understand the implications of their formative spirituality experience in view of the benefits to one's spiritual life resulting from such knowledge. The importance of spiritual formation, as related to the ministry of spiritual direction, should not be overlooked or underestimated. The well-trained and experienced director will be discerning in the process of helping each directee use the gift of art in embracing the importance of formation, conformation, and transformation in Christ.

Chapter 6

Using Art Appropriately and Effectively in Direction Sessions

"All that is true, by whomsoever it has been said, has its origin in the Spirit."

—Thomas Aquinas (1225–74)

THE PRIMACY OF SCRIPTURE IN THE MINISTRY OF SPIRITUAL DIRECTION

It is vitally important to emphasize that the use of art, in and of itself, cannot and should not be a focal point for the ministry of spiritual direction. Spiritual formation is based upon the truth of holy Scripture: the truth by which Christians are called to live. The ministry of spiritual direction is for the purpose of guiding the directee to greater knowledge and understanding of biblical truth: its meaning and call to believers for the purpose of living faithfully as disciples of Jesus Christ. Art can be a valuable asset to the ministry of spiritual direction, but only when its use is faithful to the teachings of Scripture. The use of art in spiritual direction cannot be considered as a value in and of itself, but as meaningful and useful as its use brings to the directee knowledge that is totally supportive of Scripture. The use of art is meant to encourage and inspire both spiritual director and directee in following the teachings of Jesus Christ. There are theological differences among Christian denominations and groups, and yet there are the non-negotiable Christian beliefs, doctrines, and practices such as the statements of faith as expressed in the Apostles', Nicene, and Athanasian Creeds.

Countless artists throughout Christian history have expressed religious themes in their creations. Many have tried to remain faithful to biblical truth in painting, sculpture, music, and other expressive arts. There are also artists who begin with biblical truth, adding their own interpretation to a particular passage of Scripture. Often these interpretations are very personal in that they are meant to reveal certain aspects of the artist's own life and experience: the way he or she views a religious theme or understanding of a biblical passage. In spiritual direction, it is important to consider whether or not a work of art closely adheres to a biblical representation of a person, prophecy, event, etc., or the artist has used creative license in presenting a religious topic in art. It is important for the director to discuss with a directee the degree of biblical accuracy of a particular work of art. All art is open to interpretation by the person experiencing the art. It is important that the ministry of spiritual direction always use integrity in remaining faithful to biblical truth. Otherwise, the errors in interpretation and understanding could be damaging to the spiritual formation and overall life of faith as concerns the directee. William Holman Hunt's symbolic interpretation of Revelation 3:20, "Behold, I stand at the door and knock . . . ," is seen in his painting *The Light of the World.*

The Light of the World, William Holman Hunt

Spiritual Direction in a Media-Centered Age

Historically, the ministry of spiritual direction has not included the use of art. In the present media-centered age, diverse art forms are readily available in many contexts. The use of art does not dismiss or diminish the importance of dialogue in spiritual direction sessions. However, art has the potential to enhance and enlarge dialogue and discussion, creating new dimensions in the meaning and values of the ministry. What one cannot unlock or understand through verbal discussion and verbal prayer may be opened to comprehension by engaging with various art forms during or between direction sessions.

Mediated Communication

The present era of technological communication maintains a focus on visual information. Mediated communication through the use of the internet, television, film, video, and cell phone, are forms of communication dependent primarily on persons' visual attention and abilities. One might spend hours surfing the internet or texting via cell phone while not using one's auditory abilities. Younger members of society in particular are used to visual forms of mediated communication. Therefore, there is the possibility they will be especially sensitive to the use of art, especially those purely visual forms of art, in spiritual direction.

The Importance of Sensitivity in Directing the Use of Art

Every spiritual director is unique in his or her approach to direction and therefore to the use of art in the ministry. Every directee is also unique in his or her experience with artworks, therefore, a wise director avoids a legalistic approach to the use of art. Numerous approaches are valid in using art in spiritual direction. Directors must keep in mind that every individual use of art in this ministry is a new and creative process, as led by the Holy Spirit, and should be sensitive to the personality, spirituality, preferences, and needs of the directee. Because art forms and individual works of art are extensive, it may take time for the director and directee to test the waters of art use in determining what forms, and what particular pieces of art within an individual form, may be best suited to the directee's journey in spiritual direction.

Remaining Open to the Process of Discernment

A gradual, thoughtful approach to the process is a cardinal principle in the use of art in spiritual direction. The first step is for the director and directee to carefully consider the choice of a particular art form and the specific work of art most appropriate for the directee. When artwork is chosen, the directee should not be pressured to discern any particular meaning in the art. Rather, he or she should engage with the art, looking, touching, reading, listening—whatever action is appropriate to the art form—and simply remain open to the process of discernment, just as one engages with Scripture by first reading, then moving to the processes of study, interpretation, meditation, and contemplation of Scripture. In the use of art in direction, ample time for the reflective process is required. When introduced to a particular work of art, an individual may decide whether or not he or she desires further engagement with the work, moving on to discussion, interpretation, and finally to discerning areas of meaning which may then be applied to one's life. A director must avoid leading in a way that controls the directee's experience with the art. The director's approach and attitude should be to graciously and carefully act as a supportive encourager in the process. He or she should avoid any tendency to control the directee's own experience, yet assist in the need for the process to reflect biblically supported truth. Veering from the principles of biblical truth could invalidate the meaning and value of the individual's personal engagement with an artistic work.

Although an individual may show initial enthusiasm for engaging with art, at some point he or she may decide to abandon any further interaction with the process. The choice to not engage further with the use of art may indicate a lack of enthusiasm, boredom with the process, or perhaps avoidance of certain emotions and truths stimulated by engagement with the art. Graciously discussing the directee's reason or reasons for laying aside the use of art is a wise approach. Discussion opens the direction process to reflection and prayer concerning the question Is it wise for the directee to remain open to engagement with art at another time in the direction process? In every situation where the directee no longer desires to use forms of art, the director must be careful to avoid asking the individual to press on when doing so may place them in the position of having to deal with areas of spirituality, emotional issues, and relationships they are not ready to approach, or for which counsel or therapy is needed to deal with difficult personal issues.

A Graced Process

Engaging with art in spiritual direction should be considered a graced process, never one that is forced, but approached with the idea of exploring the possible benefits of using art and offering the process prayerfully to God, with assurance that the Lord will guide both director and directee. The use of art involves prayerful reflection, discussion, and discovery as each instance of engagement with art reveals its own God-given time frame, value, and meaning to the individual's spiritual understanding.

Personal and Family Art

Directees may want to consider the use of artworks that are very personal and part of each one's spiritual journey in their families of origin. Artwork including sculptures, photographs, textile arts, and music as created by the directee, family members, or friends, often evokes strong emotions and memories related to various stages in life. These works of art may include spiritual, psychological, and emotional resonance with the directee and therefore provide important subjects for the process of engagement with art. A painting or other work of art that was displayed in one's childhood home, or art purchased at another point in life, may represent, upon reflection, significant and personal spiritual meaning. The same is true for works of art created by a family member, spouse, or friend, and therefore deserve to be included in one's ongoing engagement with art in spiritual direction. Often an individual may have previously regarded these works in a particular way, but further reflection upon the art may reveal new depths of meaning that resonate with one's deeper spiritual sensibilities, needs, and longings.

A director can help a directee by asking if he or she recalls life experiences involving artistic creations, thereby allowing a creative opportunity to engage with art in a fresh way, discovering new value and meanings in the works. A work of art need not be classic, or even well-known or heralded as a masterpiece, to be included as part of spiritual direction. Sometimes very simple works by unknown artists may stimulate spiritually significant and emotionally meaningful experiences as one engages with the art. Depending on the individual, countless works of art of all types may yield a personal response. Art that represents a thread of history in the directee's life, one that connects with a personal event or events with family or friends, may yield amazing insights into one's spiritual life, encouraging growth and maturing of relationships. If a person has access to various works of art that have been part of his or her life, and begins to interact anew with these works by viewing, touching, or hearing them again, the process may yield important results in the quest for continuing spiritual formation and growth in knowing and loving God.

Sensitivity to Individual Differences in the Use of Art

Spiritual direction must attune itself to the uniqueness of the individual, carefully considering the gender, ethnicity, culture, faith community context, and other factors relating to the most appropriate and effective use of art. For example, the exclusive use of paintings, sculpture, musical compositions, and other works created by artists of the same gender, ethnicity, culture, and Christian faith tradition, may not resonate as strongly with individuals from different backgrounds than those of the artists. Using artworks that relate well to a directee's background and perspectives may be ultimately limiting, while the use of diverse art categories and individual works that challenge the directee to perceive truth in new ways may provide the most rewarding experience. Engaging with the new and unknown, as well as the known and familiar in art, represents a balanced approach.

The importance of exploring options in various genres that include diversities of cultural and chronological contexts in art cannot be overstated. When a directee feels no resonance, emotionally or spiritually, with a work of art, connecting to the work primarily on an intellectual basis, the use of art becomes merely an academic exercise. Exploring works of art relating to the realities of an individual's spiritual journey, family of origin, gender, ethnicity, culture, and Christian tradition, enhances the process of engagement with art, adding greater value and meaning to the ministry of spiritual direction.

During engagement with art, one's preference for genres or individual works should be noted by the director. A feeling of connection with the art allows the work to have a "voice" that communicates and relates to a person's identity, life experiences, needs, hopes, dreams, goals, and emotions. This sense of connection assists the directee in recognizing what is inward and hidden, as well as what is outward and expressed in one's spirituality. However, as stated, exclusive use of artworks that relate well to a directee's background and perspectives may be somewhat limiting for the directee.

Spiritual Autobiography

One approach to the use of art in spiritual direction is for the directee to design, by freehand or via computer template, a chart tracing the chronology of his or her spiritual autobiography. The chart will serve effectively whether it is very simple or more complex in design. In creating the chart, it is necessary to note, by individual number, each year of one's life and then, from memory, place a symbol (a cross or other iconic image will do) at a particular chronological juncture, for example at five or ten-year intervals, stating briefly the event or events which were spiritually significant at each chronological juncture. After charting the most meaningful spiritual milestones, an individual may choose a particular work of art symbolizing the spiritual significance of each milestone. Another possibility is to begin by choosing a series of artworks, each one representing a spiritual milestone in the progression of one's life. One may then reflect, recording notations about each artwork's significance, not only to a singular milestone, but how the meaning of the work relates to subsequent milestones in the directee's life.

In engaging any particular exercise in spiritual direction having to do with art, one of the keys to a meaningful and valuable experience is to devote adequate time to the reflective process. Waiting in quietness with one's focus on the presence of God, and not upon the art in and of itself, while seeking the Holy Spirit to reveal the spiritual significance of the artwork, results in discovering the art's meaning and value to its viewer.

Kinesthetic Prayer

One may engage with art to express prayer, not using words, but by the kinesthetic approach of drawing, painting, molding with clay, photographing a scene, or creating a piece of music to wordlessly express the innermost intent of one's prayer.[1] One need not be a gifted artist to use a particular art media in expressing a spiritual need, inner longing, or desire to know God, as well expressing many other questions and emotions that are present in one's continuing spiritual journey of change and growth. For example, the memories evoked by photographs speak to the eternal value each moment

1. See Gerding, *Drawing to God*, and Sybil MacBeth, *Praying in Color: Drawing a New Path to God*, for further information helpful to spiritual directors and directees who desire to consider further possibilities for the use of art in spiritual direction.

in life represents, and the deep reverence with which one is called by God to be thankful for every single moment.

Another approach, which may be included with the previous, is for the directee to write or type the prayer emerging from his or her experience with the artwork, followed by verbally sharing that prayer during the direction session. Praying the same prayer during the intervening time between sessions may also yield additional insights. If so inclined, and the art form employed is music, the directee may find it meaningful and valuable to sing the prayer, as an expression of personal psalmody.

"Photography as a practice to support spiritual direction combines the active art of image-receiving with the contemplative nature and openheartedness of prayer."[2] Discerning the spiritual meaning of visual images through the guidance of the Holy Spirit is a revelatory process leading to the acknowledgement of truth.[3]

Photography is an ideal practice for those who desire to participate in the creation of artistic works that may be used as part of the contemplative life. Integrating creative expression into one's life enriches the ability to discern truth through iconic images. Reflecting upon photographic images can encourage silent worship if one is focused not the image itself, but prayerfully seeking God's truth beyond the image. When we see the world with eyes of the heart, we can engage in acts of both reverence to God and self-expression. We can discover ways in which God's creative Spirit uses the visual realm of the world to reveal truth.[4]

Keeping a Personal Journal

One way to aid individuals in expressing their responses to art, especially those who may be more reticent in sharing those responses, is to ask the directee to record a personal journal of direction sessions. Following a time of reflection and silent prayer for discernment after viewing a particular work of art, the directee may be encouraged to write down a few words, brief thoughts, or sentences concerning their experience with the work of art. The director may then invite the directee to share those written

2. Paintner, Eyes of the Heart, 3. "I pray that the eyes of your heart may be enlightened, so that you will know what is the hope of His calling, what are the riches of the glory of His inheritance in the saints . . ." (Eph 1:18 NASB).

3. Paintner, *Eyes of the Heart*, 3.

4. Paintner, *Eyes of the Heart*, 6.

reflections, one by one, and to comment further if the individual desires to share in more depth concerning the experience. This method can be especially helpful in group spiritual direction as members build trust, a spirit of openness, and sense of community with the group. The director should also invite the individual or group members to reflect further, as they continue to engage with the artwork between direction sessions. During those times, additional journaling may be encouraged, including the writing of poetry or a psalm, as one continues to engage with the artwork. Allowing a directee ample time to engage with art, followed by reflecting on the experience, provides an opportunity for deeper fellowship with the Holy Spirit to discern God's movements within the participant's mind and spirit.

A Spiritual Direction Portfolio

Directees may also find it helpful to keep a notebook, electronic or hard copy, of copyable photos from internet sites, or personally produced photos one has taken with camera or cell phone. The notebook would include written or typed reflections and prayers including the dates spent in meditative reflections on the artwork. The notebook then becomes a spiritual direction portfolio providing a permanent record of engagement with art. The portfolio allows an individual to later review their journey of using art in spiritual direction, considering truths that have emerged in the process, including how one has gained greater maturity in their Christian walk of faith.

Diverse Contexts for Artistic Engagement

It is not necessary for the director and directee to limit their shared experiences with art to direction sessions that occur in an office setting. Visiting an art museum or church, attending a concert or other event where various types of art are available, allows an individual to experience art in different contexts than in the usual meeting place for spiritual direction sessions. Viewing and reflecting on art in other settings may further enrich the process of engagement with various media. One may feel more open in expressing reactions to a work of art when in a different setting than a traditional spiritual direction context. It is not necessary for the director to accompany a directee on field visits to view artwork, nor would it always be appropriate. However, the option should be discussed and individuals encouraged to discover and reflect on engagement with art in new and unique settings.

Creativity in Spiritual Direction

For various reasons, some persons may be reticent to engage with art as part of their experience with spiritual direction. An individual may have little interest in art or feel that because he or she is not artistically gifted, they will have difficulty understanding how a particular work of art relates to their life and spirituality. In such instances, the director may provide gentle encouragement if he or she explains that the gifts of creativity in one's life are often diverse and multifaceted.

> Creativity is limited only by an undeveloped imagination. One of the challenges is to activate our ossified imagination so that our creative energies can be channeled in exciting and nourishing ways. The classics of Western spirituality are filled with images that help people understand their relationship with God: Catherine of Siena uses the image of a bridge to show the role of Christ in redemption; John of the Cross takes the image of fire in the log to symbolize the process of purgation and growth in the Lord; Teresa uses the symbol of the castle to depict the stages of spiritual development. Imagination, stimulated through analogy, deepens our knowledge of God's grace. . . .[5]

Maintaining a Balanced Approach to the Use of Art

Another consideration is how to maintain balance in direction when art is used. It is necessary to integrate the use of artistic forms with other methods in direction to ensure that each element used in the process complements other approaches.

It is important to avoid the overuse of art in spiritual direction, overwhelming the directee, and resulting in less inclination to engage in the sharing and discussion that is essential to the process. The directee should be invited gently, but with encouragement, to engage with and then express their reflections concerning a work of art. In other words, the process is "you are invited to," not "you have to." If the directee is initially uninterested

5. Morneau, *Spiritual Direction*, 117.

in the use of art, a director must respect the person's decision. It is true that engagement with art is not necessary to the process of direction, but may be meaningful and valuable when used with wisdom and discretion, as guided by the Holy Spirit.

Time for Silence and Reflection

In using art, the director must not overlook the importance of allowing adequate time for silence and reflection, beginning with viewing, touching, or hearing the work, then moving to meditation on the possible meanings of the art as personally related to the directee's life and faith. Direction sessions and the time between sessions are required to adequately experience the art and prayerfully reflect, meditate, contemplate, and journal for the purpose of understanding how the truth revealed by art relates to the directee's spiritual reality and growth in Christ.

The Importance of Silence

I remember one particular session during my training in spiritual direction when one of my peers, serving as a student director, posed a specific question to me. When I didn't answer in a few seconds, rather than talking further, the student director remained silent, allowing me sufficient time to deeply consider the question. In that silent space the question descended into my spirit as I began to realize the deeper meaning of the question and its implications for my life. I was speechless, meditating on the question in silence as the director respected my need to remain in that wordless place for several minutes. It was his willingness to allow a space for silence, and to respect that space, that allowed me the time needed to remain focused on the emotional and spiritual power of the director's question. Honoring a silent response to the use of art is one way a director shows honor, respect, patience, and compassion for the individual's needs as well as sensitivity to the Holy Spirit's movements.

Silence does not indicate a non-response but is a valid reply that may be more meaningful and powerful than a spoken response. Silences may indicate the movements of the Holy Spirit within the directee, even unspoken prayers, unuttered needs, and longings that are vitally important to the process of spiritual direction, yet cannot be expressed in words: "In the same way the Spirit also helps our weakness; for we do not know how to pray as we should, but the Spirit Himself intercedes for us with groanings too deep for words. . . ."[6]

Directors' Preparation for the Use of Art

Adequate preparation for a spiritual director includes keeping an electronic file as well as a hard copy file containing a list of facsimiles of artwork, in various media, that are suitable for spiritual direction. There are numerous websites providing excellent representations of art and its various media throughout history as well as contemporary examples. It is helpful to maintain an electronic file of these websites, and when proper copyright usage permits, to maintain a record of art photos. One may categorize and separate these files under individual headings, referring to each particular art media including paintings, sculpture, textiles, photography, musical works, and other art forms. It is helpful to include diverse choices in each category. For example, paintings should include works from a variety of historical eras and individual artists. The same would be true of each category: diversity in era, artist, and style provide more opportunities for an individual to personally relate to an artistic work. Works that express overtly religious topics as well as works of art, although seemingly secular in topic, contain subjects and themes that may speak to vitally important spiritual issues in one's life.

Individuals may also possess self-created artistic works, or meaningful works by friends and/or family members, that may be used to engage with art in the process of spiritual direction. The director will need to interview the directee to determine what type or types of art media or particular works of art he or she would choose for engagement in the process of prayerful reflection and contemplation while using creative works.

A Director's Sensitivity and Discernment

The director needs a careful, sensitive approach in guiding individuals through the process of engagement with artistic works. Directors should always consider the directee's preference in the choice of art. A person is often drawn to a work of art because, on a conscious or subconscious level, the art resonates with their innermost thoughts, feelings, longings,

6. Rom 8:16.

desires, and memories. One cannot overestimate the power of art to touch the deep recesses of one's being if the process of engagement with art is guided by the Holy Spirit. An individual is vulnerable in the process of including artistic works in the ministry of spiritual direction because strong memories and intense feelings may be evoked during engagement with art. These strong responses may represent an expression, for the first time, of repressed memories or emotions. An expressed response to art may bring a catharsis, a process of cleansing, and ultimately healing, in a particular area of spiritual need. A director must use sensitivity and discernment in understanding an individual's spiritual and emotional needs: an important reason why engagement with art should not be introduced in the initial stages of spiritual direction.

Engaging the Whole Person

The process of spiritual direction has the potential to engage the whole person: intellect, spirit, will, and body. One example of this holistic engagement is the spiritual exercise known as Stations of the Cross. The exercise is often conducted outdoors where individual stations related to the Passion of Jesus Christ have been set up at various distances to one another. Remaining in a spirit of prayer, one walks to each station which includes a statement and/or Scriptural passage referring to a single event of Jesus' Passion. The statements are often carved or painted on wood, which may include additional related carvings, sculptures, or paintings that serve as visual representations of each phase in Christ's Passion. This spiritual exercise is familiar to various Christian traditions in the liturgical-sacramental stream of theology and practice.[7]As a participant walks to each station, reading the various Scriptures, and prayerfully reflecting on the content of each station's meaning to his or her own life, one experiences the art forms in ways that engage the whole person. I experienced an inspiring representation of Stations of the Cross at Shrine Mont Conference and Retreat Center, Orkney Springs, Virginia.[8] In this beautiful mountainous

7. Stations of the Cross, also called *Via Crucis*, Way of the Cross or Way of Sorrows, dating to the fourth century and originated by Christians who desired to walk, as an act of devotion, the pathway originally traveled by Jesus Christ during the journey of his passion.

8. Located in Orkney Springs, VA, Shrine Mont is the conference and retreat center for the Episcopal Diocese of Virginia.

area, the stations, with their carved wood plaques identifying each phase of the Passion, are mounted on various trees. The stations are visual in their artwork, yet invite touch, for one may feel the carvings of Scripture on each station's plaque. Breathing the mountain air, one may listen to the singing birds and the sounds of animals emanating from the dense woods, and hear the crunching sounds of one's steps along the mountain trail where the plaques are located. As one ascends the trail, one eventually arrives at a high wooden tower where a large white cross is mounted on an open platform, surrounded by safety railings, at the tower's apex. One may walk the steps to the top of the tower and then, looking outward, contemplate the extensive view, extending for miles and miles, of God's stunning forest and mountain landscape.

Walking the Stations of the Cross at Shrine Mont is a specific use of spiritual direction, as each of the actual stations, with its respective carvings and Scriptures, becomes the "director" for the person engaged in the exercise. Both the Scriptures and the artistic representations of Jesus' suffering urge the pilgrim on to each subsequent station, inviting the participant to open mind and heart, to renew and deepen their knowledge and understanding of Jesus' Passion. In this use of art in spiritual direction, the actual stations themselves are directing the pilgrim, by speaking through the Scriptures, nature, and the walking journey, urging the seeker on to the next station while encouraging prayerful reflection on the sufferings of Christ. It is a formative walk as one interacts with the reality of Christ's salvific journey on behalf of humankind, an encounter with the words of truth proclaiming the Lord's sacrifice. When art connects us with the reality of the living Christ, then art has accomplished the fullest of its creative purposes, informing, changing, enriching our spiritual lives, and freeing us to move lovingly forward in serving God and others. This type of interaction with art allows a strong kinesthetic focus for participants as well as visual and auditory participation resulting in a full and substantive experience in individual or group spiritual direction.

Accommodating Special Needs

For directees who are disabled or for group spiritual direction when an outdoor walking version of stations of the cross is not doable due to inclement weather or other limitations, it is possible for participants to enjoy a similar experience indoors. Participants may gather together in a suitable indoor space for the activity. The spiritual director will need to provide framed artistic prints or photographs of each station representing Jesus' Passion. I have used this format with success for a group of approximately twelve individuals who participated with me in a healing conference interactive workshop titled "An Hour in the Presence of Jesus." This visual, contemplative, and formational workshop, based on the Gospels' accounts of the Passion of Christ, was developed to provide workshop participants with a personal and experiential opportunity to explore the events of Jesus' life as these events have meaning and application to the ministry of Christian healing for the whole person.

The goal of the workshop concerned providing an opportunity for participants to experience the reality of each station's scenario; its history and message, to encourage attendees' personal and dynamic connection with the events of Jesus' Passion. The artwork used for this workshop consisted of several large, framed, color photographs depicting events from the film *The Passion of the Christ*. Seated in a circle, participants were given each photograph, one at a time, as they observed silence. Individuals held each framed photo, allowing time for reflection on the image presented before handing the photo to the next person in the circle. As director of the group, I read a single passage from Scripture relating to individual photographs. Participants, prior to the workshop, had previously received a ten-page written guide to the workshop outlining each phase of the session. The guide included Scriptures, a reflection statement for each Scripture, a written prayer, and an invitation to engage in a period of silence after each photo had processed through the group. Although this particular context of direction involved a group setting, it is possible to present the same scenario for direction in a one-to-one setting. This particular workshop format integrates reflection and prayer, with engagement in an art form, to provide a rich context for spiritual direction.

Spiritual growth affects the whole person, influencing, encouraging, and even completing needed healing in the emotional, physical, and relational areas of life. The workshop's visual, meditative approach to remembering Jesus' Passion through paintings, sculpture, or photographs from the film previously mentioned, emphasize the reality of Christ's body and blood, given and shed for all who would receive these measureless, eternal gifts. It is essential for director and directee to understand the meditative approach to Scripture through art. The events described in the biblical record present powerful symbols. Employed properly in spiritual direction, reflection on the meaning of those symbols encourages progress in one's unfolding journey of healing and one's desire for wholeness in Christ Jesus.

Using Art with Care and Discernment

Ministry is enhanced by those directors who understand and apply the various uses of art in direction, employing its resources to best advantage, with care and discretion in appropriate ways and at appropriate times in a person's spiritual journey. It is important for the director to learn the directee's level of appreciation for art and their experience with various art forms. For example, which art forms most resonate with the person: is it painting, sculpture, music, or some other art form? Questions to ask: Are you drawn to a particular form or specific work of art? Are you open to exploring this form of artistic expression? Is there a particular work of art that has previously sparked your interest and therefore bears further exploration as part of direction? Does the particular work of art evoke your spiritual affections, ideas, attitudes or longings?" These and other questions should be addressed with sensitivity and discernment. It is important for a director to become acquainted with a person's goals for spiritual direction and to gain an understanding of the directee's spiritual life. This information will reveal whether or not the introduction of art as part of direction has potential as a meaningful and valuable resource to one's spiritual life and growth.

A single work of art may represent a major theme in one's spiritual life. It is not the number of art forms or works used in direction, but the spiritual meaning and value of each work that determines the effectiveness of the use of art. A single artistic work may be used for a period of weeks or months, or it may become an overarching theme for the duration of the person's engagement in spiritual direction. Several works of art, all of which express the same theme, can be helpful because the theme may be experienced in various artistic contexts and in different genres of art. For example, a painting depicting prayer may be the starting point for eventual engagement with sculpture depicting a similar theme, or a piece of music, a dance, or drama concerning the theme of prayer. A spiritual director is wise to proceed slowly, using one piece of art at a time while making sure the directee's interaction with the artwork has concluded before moving on to the use of other works. Spiritual direction requires sensitivity, discernment, and patience on the part of the director to avoid interference with the movements and timing of the Holy Spirit. As the primary director, the

Spirit's movements and timings must not only be discerned but followed for maximum effect in the ministry of direction.

Dimensions of Faith

One challenge in the journey of continuing spiritual maturation is contending with both the practical realities of living in the three-dimensional world, and the realities of the unseen dimension of the Spirit, the realm of reality sometimes defined as the mystery of God or apophatic Christian spirituality. Both God-revealed and God-concealed—these two dimensions of reality—are important to the context of spiritual direction. One cannot understand or deal with the earthly dimensions of life without an appreciation for, and willingness to embrace, the reality of faith which acknowledges another dimension of life. Faith is the substance and evidence through which we discern the movements of God, allowing us to believe and act on the reality of God's presence in our lives and in the lives of others. This felt tension, the reality of living in one dimension yet embracing the reality of unseen dimensions, cannot be overlooked or underestimated as a primary spiritual and practical tension in the ministry of spiritual direction.

God makes his presence and unfailing love known through the gift of creation. The good things of God's creation effectively enhance the spiritual lives of individuals and faith communities. A mystical understanding of God's love in Christ—"For God so loved the world, that He gave His only begotten Son, that whoever believes in Him shall not perish, but have eternal life"[9]—may be expressed in artistic works. It is the eternal love of the Father, Son, and Spirit, in perfect community, that humankind seeks, whether or not individuals are aware that God's love is each person's deepest need. Through the window of art, and by the power of the Spirit, it is possible to connect with the reality of this ultimate need and longing for God. A work of art can clearly speak in silence about what we most desire and yet often seems to elude our grasp. When a work of art is authentic in what it expresses, then its reality moves one's mind and spirit, perhaps with some level of resistance to truth on our part, to acknowledge one's most profound human need to know and worship God.

The reality of God may be acknowledged in sermons, studied in meditation on the Scriptures, and contemplated in works of art created for

9. John 3:16 NASB.

the glory of God. A work of art has the ability to provide a witness to the redemptive power of Jesus Christ. All forms of art may be used evangelistically in speaking to the ever-present human need to fill one's spiritual void, redeeming one's lostness and assuaging one's longing for spiritual reality. When art is a creative expression of Scripture, when art communicates the truth of the gospel, then it is united with the one reality of God's truth and has the ability to speak that truth to our eyes, ears, minds, emotions, and spirits. Just as Scripture reveals God's ultimate message of love and redemption, art also reveals profound visions of truth in powerful ways. In spiritual direction, the use of art has the redemptive purpose to inform, to teach, and through the Holy Spirit, to transform one's understanding and one's character. When a specific work of art is true to the witness of God as revealed in Scripture, then it has the power to witness redemptively to the meaning and value of each life, and to those communities seeking the divine truth of relationship with God as revealed in Jesus Christ. Spiritual direction is a journey in learning to perceive the movements of God in one's life, in learning the ways of prayer, and growing in faith and spiritual maturity. It is not uncommon that one may experience blockages in spiritual understanding during direction when the tool of communication between the director and directee is limited to discussion. For many, discussion alone may yield understanding and transformation. One must also consider that the use of art may potentially encourage a depth of understanding for the directee that discussion alone cannot accomplish.

The Physical Senses in Spiritual Direction

Although Scripture is the most important focal point for guidance in the ministry of spiritual direction, visual, tactile, or auditory stimulation through art can evoke or encourage prayer, memories, insights, desires, and illuminate truth, as well as encourage the process of healing and other emotional and intellectual responses related to spiritual life. Physical senses have the capacity to enlarge one's understanding of God, the self, and others. Visual images often speak to needs and situations in one's life, while helping an individual perceive needed insights concerning personal relationships and the need to clarify the meaning of emotional responses. Engaging with artistic works can be helpful in processing grief events, for art often evokes personal memories. A sensitive spiritual director understands when and when not to use various art forms during direction. It is important not to overwhelm a directee with visual, tactile, or auditory stimulation through art, but to carefully assist the directee in finding a particular work of art that resonates with his or her own life experiences: those personal events the directee finds relevant and is willing to explore. When an art form and a specific work are engaged in the process of direction, then it is helpful to stay with the selection for a while, companioning the directee as various meanings derived from the work are explored.

Visual stimulation results in various levels of emotional responses. For example, if an individual is struggling with repressed emotions, art, as used by the Holy Spirit, has power to reveal emotions to one's consciousness where they can be felt and acknowledged. Prayerful personal reflection, followed by acknowledging the presence of those emotions with one's director, may move the directee to greater self-understanding which serves as an important aspect in the process of spiritual, emotional, and relational healing.

The primary goal for the use of art in spiritual direction is, of course, spiritual growth. However, emotional, physical, or spiritual healing cannot be separated from the process of spiritual growth. Therefore, working through the process of reflecting on artwork to gain insights and understanding from that process, will always benefit one's need for healing and wholeness. We often try to deny or hide from our sins, from those ways we are not Christlike. Engagement with art can serve as a means to arouse and encourage one's desire to grow in grace, as one becomes more aware of personal sin, and becomes more sensitive to the Holy Spirit's presence and guidance in the daily walk of faith.

Visuality in Spiritual Direction

Spiritual direction is saved from a one-dimensional approach, and becomes much more sensitive to the needs of the directee, when art is added to the ministry. Visuality is a gift and an ability by which one relates to God, to the world, and to others; it is part of worship, of interacting with others while serving in one's vocation. For the director to simply ask the directee the question: What are you seeing in everyday life that speaks to your relationship with God? can begin an important conversation concerning the use of various art forms, and why interaction with these forms are beneficial to the directee's life and faith development.

Artwork as a form of mediated communication allows the Spirit of God to reveal God's self to the directee through the messages conveyed by visuality or other senses used in engagement with art. Rembrandt's *The Return of the Prodigal* Son silently symbolizes the reality of God the Father's steadfast and forgiving love. Michelangelo's *Pietà* reveals the tenderness and compassion of Mary's grieving love for the suffering and death of her Son. The visuality of art emphasizes the reality of Scripture, communicating additional dimensions of meaning and new ways of "seeing" the biblical message that opens one's understanding, and encourages the application of an active faith to one's life.

A Process of Patience and Prayer

In a technologically advanced era, people are constantly barraged with countless visual images and auditory stimuli through media. Individuals are not always aware that overexposure to sensual stimulation may limit or dull the value of using art in spiritual direction. Spiritual direction requires time to understand the deeper meaning of what is received and processed using one's senses, intellect, and spirit. Sensory overload can dull one's ability to receive the rich potential of engagement with various art forms. The reflective process as one engages with a painting, photograph, sculpture, textile art, or musical work requires openness to the art form. The process also requires patience and prayer, as one considers the artwork's symbolism, its meaning to the viewer or listener, and the emerging thoughts and emotions that engagement with the work reveals. These revelations open an individual to the holy mystery of God as well as the unfolding revelation of God's presence in an individual life. Important to consider in the use of art is a work's balance of apophatic spirituality (the mystery of God) and kataphatic spirituality (God's revelation of God's self): does the work emphasize one or the other, or are both expressed in the subject, message, and other aspects of the work?

A Ministry for All

Spiritual direction must be considered as a ministry available to all, not limited to persons with a certain level of intellect, or the full abilities of the physical senses. With sensitivity and creativity by the director, spiritual direction is possible, in one form or another, for most individuals with a disability or impairment, including individuals with multiple disabilities or impairments. It is the work of the spiritual director to find the means of artistic expression that may be employed as appropriate resources for the process of spiritual direction. The gifts of God for the spiritual life, including spiritual direction, are limited only by the level of discernment and creativity on the part of the director in understanding the needs of each directee.

Art for the Visually or Auditorily Impaired

What is true of visually mediated art forms may also generally apply to one, two, and three-dimensional art forms. Most art forms, with the exception of music, require a visual approach. For the low-visioned or blind, three-dimensional art forms, and musical art forms provide the inner visions of truth necessary for spiritual direction. For those with hearing loss, visuality in art and three-dimensional art forms, such as sculpture, which allow the use of touch in exploring the artwork, can serve as powerful resources in stimulating the desire to grow in relationship with God. It is important to note that those with hearing loss can sense the vibrations arising from music, a capability not to be overlooked by the director in ministering to those with auditory challenges. Art forms appropriate to those who have certain physical needs may be used in direction to deepen one's understanding of the inner life, an understanding essential to spiritual direction.

Visuality, the ability to discern or perceive persons or objects normally perceived by physical vision, is not limited to the sighted. A person with visual loss, if formerly sighted, may "see" mental images; therefore, art forms can be described, sculptures and textiles felt, music heard, and the essence of various colors explained by director to directee. For those individuals who do not see mental images when thinking, praying, or reading, art allows a new and needed dimension to their growth in prayer and to discerning the Spirit's presence and movements in their lives.

The blind have visually related abilities, for example, sight memory, or "seeing" through touch or by means of verbal descriptions. A director can describe a work of art to the low-visioned or blind and, if possible, allow the person to touch the work, to feel the temperature of the canvas, the smoothness or roughness of a sculpture, the size of the work or the texture created by a weaver, or an artist's brush strokes, for example. The contents of a photograph may be described verbally. The visually impaired who have auditory abilities, are fully open to artistic works in music, film, recordings, or books, and other works of art which include the element of sound. Those who are sighted but have hearing loss will need a director proficient in sign language or may invite a friend or mentor communicative in sign language to join direction sessions. For those with both visual and hearing losses,, the use of touch and signing, with interpreter if needed, will provide opportunities for communicating the spiritual dimensions associated with the use of art.

Group Contexts for Spiritual Direction

Art is rarely created for one person but for a specific group or general audience. Therefore, the use of art integrates particularly well into group spiritual direction contexts. The use of art in group situations allows members the advantages of a shared focus. Often the group process of reflecting on artistic works is especially helpful to more reticent or introverted members who receive encouragement from others' support and sharing of reflections. The group process, if directed with care and sensitivity, fosters confidence in sharing as well as a sense of community. These qualities accord the reticent person a sense of trust and a feeling of freedom to express previously unexpressed ideas and perceptions about the art.

Group direction provides a rich context for the use of artistic works. By patient reflection when engaging with artwork, each group member, in addition to his or her own shared comments concerning the work, also receives insights from the shared reflections of others in the group. There may be significant variations within any group as to how a work of art is perceived. These diversities of perception provide a wealth of insights for others in the group to consider, including sensitivity to the thoughts and opinions of others as they interact with artistic works. Just as in worship each person lends his or her own particular voice to hymns and songs of praise, in group spiritual direction each person provides his or her own perceptive "voice" to the process of engagement with artwork. In fact, it may be the shared reflections of one group member that provide the greatest insights to another person or persons in the group. In the body of Christ, it is the shared wisdom and understanding of all members, based on biblical truth, which are essential to spiritual growth and to increasing sensitivity in discerning the needs of others. The group process encourages members' ability to maturely express Christian love toward others.

Differentiating the Use of Art in Spiritual Direction with Art Therapy

It is essential for spiritual directors to understand that using art in spiritual direction cannot be equated with the practice of art therapy. Although the use of art in spiritual direction can result in benefits to emotional health, the use of artistic works in spiritual direction is not to be understood as a therapeutic approach, for the purpose of addressing emotional problems and needs. Art therapy practitioners require specific expertise to identify and understand various emotional needs and mental illnesses. The practice of art therapy requires professionals who have completed the requisite education and experience essential to the use of art in a therapeutic context.

The Need for Referral

The use of art in spiritual direction may often evoke emotional responses. The responses may relate to events in a person's early history, hurts or traumas that have not been healed and thus remain hidden or denied, with emotional defenses built to surround and protect difficult and traumatic memories and their inherent pain. An emotional response to art may also relate to more recent or current events in an individual's life. Spiritual directors should maintain constant awareness in looking for signs indicating a directee requires referral. A qualified spiritual director requires adequate education and training to recognize a directee's need for referral to a qualified counselor, psychologist, or physician to diagnosis and treat certain conditions for the purpose of emotional change and growth.

Because engagement with art is often emotionally evocative, a spiritual director brings a greater degree of safety to the relationship if he or she is informed when a directee is undergoing therapeutic treatment for mental or emotional issues or illness. At the beginning of the director-directee relationship it is important for the director to know if the individual is undergoing psychological or psychiatric therapy or is taking prescribed medications that affect thinking and emotions. Although it would be unethical to press for such information, the director can indicate that this information will be helpful to the process of direction and that all information shared with the director will be held in complete confidence. Ideally, spiritual direction will be more effective if the director receives permission from the directee to check with his or her therapist and/or physician to ascertain whether or not the directee's caregiver(s) affirm that the process of spiritual direction will be helpful to that person at their particular stage in treatment.

An individual I knew was meeting with a therapist for issues involving depression, and under his medical physician's care. He was also meeting with his pastor for spiritual counsel. Therapist, medical doctor, and pastor were aware of one another's particular role in his life and were in agreement that each one's role was essential and helpful in this individual's healing process. The ministry of spiritual direction also became one of the supportive links for the purpose of healing and wholeness in this individual's life.

Ministerial Standards for Spiritual Directors

Those who seek spiritual direction need to ascertain that the director they have chosen is well-qualified and ethical in all practices, for the ministry requires the directee's openness and therefore implies vulnerability because he or she is sharing sensitive information. In view of the nature of spiritual direction, only persons who are educated, trained, vetted, and approved by the authorities in their religious denominations or other oversight groups are prepared to engage ethically in the ministry of spiritual direction. No individual should attempt to provide the ministry of direction without the oversight and accountability factor of a qualified supervisor who is also accountable to the particular authorities of his or her ecclesial or parachurch group.

It is understood as a first principle of ministry that one should never provide a ministry or perform a ministry that one is not also receiving as part of their accountability in ministry. For example, pastors need pastoring, counselors need counseling, prophets need others to speak prophetically into their lives, teachers need the lifelong discipline of continuing education, and spiritual directors need the ministry of other directors and those qualified to serve as supervisors in the ministry.

Preparing for the Use of Art in Spiritual Direction

Prior to the introduction of art forms, the directee should receive a full explanation of the purposes, expectations, and goals for engagement with artistic works. The director should obtain the full consent of the directee, with his or her affirmation that the purposes and goals of spiritual direction are understood. Only then may art be added to the process of direction. The directee should be allowed to choose from a diverse variety of art forms and specific examples that are of interest. In this way, the directee maintains ownership of the process and is free to select particular works of art to explore. A director must avoid an authoritarian or heavy-handed approach by making choices that are best left to the discernment of the one directed. Spiritual directors should avoid trying to exert control over the process, while graciously providing an explanatory invitation as to the options and benefits in using art. Using this approach, the directee is not coerced in any way, even subtly, to include art, but maintains the freedom necessary for integrity in the process of direction. As with every approach to spiritual direction, the Holy Spirit is always the true director: both directee and director must remain aware of the Spirit's presence and open to the Spirit's guidance. In this way, the choice to use art remains a gracious invitation; an opportunity offered with the freedom to explore the options available in art.

The wise spiritual director will never underestimate the power of art, through the Holy Spirit's presence, to assist an individual in discerning truths about his or her life and spirituality, so these truths may be explored, shared, and understood within the context of spiritual direction. Art forms should be used with discretion, and only after the director carefully assesses whether or not the use of art will serve as a viable and important choice for an individual's spiritual journey in direction. Introducing the use of art too soon in the direction process, or introducing diverse and numerous types of various art forms may, rather than enhancing the ministry of spiritual direction, lead to the psychological and spiritual "overload" that is destructive to the process.

Spiritual Direction as a Lifelong Journey

The ministry of direction is understandably a lifelong journey, not a sprint into spiritual growth. Although both director and directee may agree on general and specific goals for the ministry of direction, each participant requires a spirit of openness and submission to the Holy Spirit's own perfect timing as the ministry process unfolds. It is wise to remember that art is not a necessity in spiritual direction. Art may be included to great advantage in the directee's spiritual journey, yet, as with any ministry resource, the introduction of art must be used carefully, with discernment as to an individual's needs and goals in direction. If a directee initially responds positively to the use of art, then continuing engagement with artistic works should be considered. The ministry of direction calls for different approaches at different times; too much or too little use of art may be detrimental in one way or another, depending on the particular personality and spiritual needs of the one directed.

Discerning Various Responses

Although art may sometimes stimulate strong responses, both intellectually and emotionally from the directee, these responses are not necessarily indicative of needing referral for pastoral or psychological counseling, psychiatric care, or other forms of help. However, the director must be careful and very discerning in allowing the one directed sufficient time, as well as intellectual and emotional space, to process those emotions as related to the use of art. This process, to be effective, requires patience. Art may elicit an interior knowing including new information, an epiphany, or other dynamic response. Such responses become conscious not solely due to the art itself, but because the Holy Spirit is present in the process, employing the art in creative ways to enlighten the directee's journey of faith and growth. Directors should not move quickly from one example of art to another, but practice listening skills including patience, quietness, and sensitivity, as a directee explores the meaning and value gained from his or her engagement with art.

The Directee: Types of Personal Engagement with Art

In using a specific work of art for spiritual direction, it is important to realize that the directee should not be rushed through the process. Engagement with the artwork may occur during one, or over several sessions with the director. If the artwork is particularly evocative, it is important for the directee to engage with the artwork at various times between sessions. Engagement at home with the artwork is best accompanied by the discipline of journaling, and then sharing those thoughts and impressions at the next direction session.

The directee may engage further with art by creating a personal artistic vision in painting, sculpture, music, photography, or other art forms. If the directee has not previously engaged in creative art forms, the director's encouraging invitation to do so can add layers of meaning and value to the ministry of spiritual direction. If the directee has previously created some form of art, then inviting him or her to engage further with a personally created work may further enrich the person's experience in spiritual direction.

It is important for the spiritual director to ascertain the particular type or types of art that resonate intellectually and spiritually with a directee. After the art genre is chosen, the director and directee may discuss a specific choice to begin the process of engagement with art. The director creates a more welcoming atmosphere during the process by allowing the directee to choose the type and specific example to be used. Once engagement with art has begun, the director will better understand the value of the process for the directee. From this perspective the director may suggest, for the purpose of spiritual reflection, other art forms or particular art pieces similar to the type of art the directee has chosen. It is essential that the use of art reflect an open and graced process, understanding that the Spirit of God is always the prime director; those involved in direction need to discern and follow his guidance. If the directee indicates resistance to using art, the director may carefully and gently explain why art may be beneficial, and invite the directee to try the process. If there is still resistance, then it is best to respect the decision of the directee. There may be other opportunities, at a later time, to restate a gentle invitation to engage with art when this seems appropriate in the direction process.

Encouraging the Reflective Process

Many of the following questions may elicit emotional responses. Asking the directee to deal with too many questions during one session can be overwhelming. Not every question may be valuable or appropriate and therefore should be deleted from the process. It is best to enter into and continue the process slowly to allow the directee time to fully examine, reflect upon, and respond to each question. There are times when a question does not need a response; rather, the directee needs time to pray and to reflect about the question, waiting until another time to provide a response. If the artwork chosen is not eliciting responses that are helpful to the directee, then it is wise to engage with another artwork of the same, or perhaps a different genre of art. Because this process is subjective, it is therefore unique to each person. The director's goal concerns fostering an atmosphere in which the

Holy Spirit's presence and movements will be evident to the directee in the process of engagement with art, encouraging development in discernment about one's spiritual life and growth.

Questions for Reflection

The following questions are options for spiritual direction sessions in which various genres of art are used:

Are you familiar with the artwork, or is this your first engagement with the work? If you have encountered the work at other times in your life, discuss the context of the encounter.

Describe, in your own words, the artist's subject.

What is your understanding of the message the artist wants to convey through his or her creation?

What materials has the artist used in creating the artwork?

Describe the color palette of the artwork. What emotion or emotions does the color palette convey to you?

What does the texture of the work of art convey to you?

What is the overall mood conveyed by the artwork?

Is there is an individual or group of people represented in the work? Describe each one. Describe the actions and emotions each person represented appears appear to convey.

If the artwork does not contain human figures or still life, but abstract figures or other representations using various methods and materials, what themes, thoughts, and emotions do you think the artist is attempting to convey?

What does the lighting in the artwork convey to you?

What thoughts and emotions do you think the artist was feeling during the creation of the artwork?

Do you think the artwork was created for a general or a specific audience? Explain.

Does the art invite you to enter into engagement with the piece? If not, what about the piece seems uninviting to you?

Do you discern any particular spiritual meaning as conveyed by the work?

As you continue engaging with the work, what are the thoughts and feelings you are experiencing as evoked by the art? Describe them.

Does the artwork help you to connect with the reality of your own spiritual life? If so, describe that connection.

Does the artwork represent to you a specific thought, event, or message relating to your spiritual life? If so, what is that thought, event, or message?

If you could speak now to the artist, what would you say to him or to her in describing the meaning of this artwork to you, particularly its meaning to your spiritual life?

As you continue to engage with the artwork, how would you describe its connection to your interpersonal and intrapersonal environments, your relationships, and your vocation?

What does this artwork reveal or "speak" to you about your life of prayer?

What does the artwork reveal or speak to you concerning your engagement with God through worship?

What does the artwork reveal or speak to you about your spiritual service to God and to others?

Describe your understanding of the major theme the Holy Spirit is revealing to you, through this particular artwork?

Do you sense that God is calling you to do something, or to change or grow in any particular way through what you have learned in the process of reflecting on the artwork?

After having processed through engagement with the artwork, what prayer will you offer to God?

Combining Art Forms in Spiritual Direction

Directors may wonder if various art forms may be combined, or is it best practice to use only one art form at a time before moving on to others? For example, if a particular painting is chosen as the subject for reflection and if there are other art forms that align closely in subject and feeling with the first artwork being used, is it appropriate to include other forms to represent a linkage of similar themes and ideas, all relating to the original artwork? Yes, an individual has the advantage of considering a single theme or idea as expressed through the nuances of more than one form of art, comparing and contrasting how each form expresses a similar theme or idea.

Engagement with Art: Importance of the Physical Senses

Another advantage of using various art forms in spiritual direction relates to the importance of the physical senses. Engagement with paintings requires sight, sculpture requires sight as well as touch, music requires hearing, textile art requires both sight and touch, and so forth. By engaging with several art forms, the directee can experience more of art's potential to enrich spiritual direction. Using several forms of art also allows the ministry of direction to align with what one experiences naturally in life, which is engagement with diverse forms of art at various times. Although one's preferred way of engaging with art may be through sight, touch, or hearing, using more than one physical sense, when possible, while engaging with different forms of art, enriches the experience.

One way people experience the world is through the use of the physical senses. God speaks to us in our spirits, but often that message is received initially through the entrance gate of one or more of the physical senses. The Holy Spirit uses what we see with the eyes to help us understand and interpret the profound truths of life, spirituality, and eternity. The physical, intellectual, and spiritual dimensions of life are integral in allowing one to accurately perceive truth. The Scriptures indicate that God often communicates through the avenues of one's physical senses to reveal truths to individuals, groups, and nations. Therefore, the director does well by encouraging the use of several forms of art in spiritual direction. It is often the directee's least examined or least understood art form that may yield new perspectives on life and truth, because a little-known form may bring originality and freshness to the directee's outlook and ways of thinking as they engage with art.

For example, Frederico Barroci's *The Birth of Christ* (1597) may be compared and contrasted with the marble relief sculpture of the birth of Jesus housed in Saint Mark's Basilica, Venice, Italy. The former work may be further compared and contrasted with Johann Sebastian Bach's *Christmas Oratorio* (1734).[10] These diverse art forms each bring a unique perspective

10. J. S. Bach, *Christmas Oratorio*, 1-23.

to the reality of the Messiah's birth. Each artist's singular interpretation of the birth of Jesus, according to the Gospel of Luke, allows the directee to consider the event from the perspective of personal interpretation and from the vision and the musical sense of the artists. Considering both perspectives guides the directee's perceptions of the Messiah's birth event and how it relates to personal life and spirituality. The directee has the advantage of seeing or hearing the expressions of artists who are passionate in sharing their own insights and interpretations of life and faith. For example, artistic works depicting the birth of Jesus stimulate one's thoughts and imagination to reflect upon the historical reality of the event, and its profound impact on the present-day life of the directee. However, it is always necessary that one's perspectives and perceptions of art be carefully checked with the reality of all that Scripture reveals, historically and theologically, concerning any subject or event. Scripture passages related to artwork are an important part of the process to understand and explain the significance of an artistic work to one's life and growth in faith. The artist's own explanation and understanding of his or her created work may be theologically sound, or may result in only the artist's personal interpretation, one that is not necessarily aligned with biblical truth.

> The words *explain* and *understand* . . . have very different meanings. One can argue that only artists can *explain* their work, can make intelligible something that is not known or not understood. But *understanding* is defined as full awareness or knowledge that is achieved through an intellectual or emotional process—including the ability to extract meaning or to interpret. The ability to *appreciate* or to perceive the value or worth of something from a discriminating perspective, then, is the consummate reward of understanding.[11]

Through the process of reflection, a directee is able to understand the artist's vision in portraying a particular subject or subjects. By understanding the artist's vision, a directee can interpret the work's meaning in a personal way: how he or she interprets the subject differently, and yet in the light of the artist's perception, always comparing that perception with sound biblical understanding. This process is an advantage in spiritual direction, helping to balance both objectivity and subjectivity in the interpretation of artistic works. In using art, it is important not to allow the process to become inwardly focused. Engagement with art calls one to consider the

11. Fichner-Rathus, *Understanding Art*, xiv.

viewpoints of the artists: for example, how they view spiritual life, and the ways their interpretations may allow the directee to see and understand his or her own spiritual life with more clarity. However, in using art, the spiritual director should consider whether the artist's work encourages a new depth of knowledge one that aligns with an accurate understanding of Scripture.

Bibliography

THE FOLLOWING LIST IS a compilation of cited works and relevant full resources in various art media for spiritual directors, their supervisors, and directees, as they seek information and resources for use in the ministry of spiritual direction.

Ahlborn, Mel. *Visio Divina: A Reader in Faith and Visual Arts*. Leeds, MA: LeaderResources, 2009.

Athnos, Gregory S. *The Art of the Roman Catacombs: Themes of Deliverance in an Age of Persecution*. Parker, CO: Outskirts, 2011.

Bach, J. S. "Christmas Oratorio." Choral Score by S. Jadassohn. English version. Van Nuys, CA: Alfred Music, 1985.

Barbe-Gall, Françoise. *How to Look at a Painting*. London: Francis Lincoln Limited, 2011.

Bauer, Michael J. *Arts Ministry: Nurturing the Creative Life of God's People*. Grand Rapids: Eerdmans, 2013.

Beckett, Sister Wendy. *A Child's Book of Prayer in Art*. New York: DK, 1995.

———. *Sister Wendy on the Art of Mary*. Cincinnati: Franciscan Media, 2013.

———. *Sister Wendy on the Art of Saints*. Cincinnati: Franciscan Media, 2011.

Beckman, Betsey, and Christine Valters Paintner. *Awakening the Creative Spirit: Bringing the Arts to Spiritual Direction*. Harrisburg: Morehouse, 2010.

Bell, Kathryn L. *Our Christian Heritage in Art*. Greenville, SC: BJU, 1999.

Benner, Juliet. *Contemplative Vision: A Guide to Christian Art and Prayer*. Downers Grove: InterVarsity, 2011.

Benson, Bruce Ellis, and James Smith. *Liturgy as a Way of Life: Embodying the Arts and Christian Worship*. Grand Rapids: Baker Academic, 2013.

Best, Harold M. *Unceasing Worship: Biblical Perspectives on Worship and the Arts*. Downers Grove: InterVarsity, 2003.

Bittigole, Michael, and James D. Childs. *Catholic Spirit: An Anthology for Discovering Faith Through Literature, Art, Film and Music*. Notre Dame, IN: Ave Maria, 2010.

Blain, Susan A., ed. *Imaging the Word: An Arts and Lectionary Resource*. Vol 2. Cleveland: United Church Press, 1995.

Bowden, Sandra. *Faith and Vision: Twenty-Five Years of Christians in the Visual Arts*. Baltimore: Square Halo, 2005.

Bowles, Jon. *Art and Faith: Reclaiming the Artistic Essence of the Church*. Kansas City: The House Studio, 2012.

Brand, Hilary, and Adrienne Chaplin. *Art and Soul: Signposts for Christians in the Arts.* 2nd ed. Downers Grove: IVP Academic, 2001.
Brown, Ann. *Apology to Women: Christian Images of the Female Sex.* Leicester, UK: InterVarsity, 1991.
Brown, Michael P. *The Lion Companion to Christian Art.* Oxford, UK: Lion Hudson, 2008.
Burckhardt, Titus. *The Foundations of Christian Art.* Bloomington, IN: World Wisdom, 2006.
Burke, Daniel, and John Bartunek. *Navigating the Interior Life: Spiritual Direction and the Journey to God.* Steubenville, OH: Emmaus, 2012.
Campbell, Joseph. *Thou Art That: Transforming Religious Metaphor.* Novato, CA: New World Library, 2001.
Christie, Yves, and Velman Christie. *Art of the Christian World A.D. 200–1500: A Handbook of Styles and Forms.* New York: Rizzoli International, 1982.
Collins, Kristen, Peter Kidd, and Nancy Turner. *The Saint Albans Psalter: Painting and Prayer in Medieval England.* Los Angeles: J. Paul Getty Museum, 2013.
Couchman, Judith. *A Guide to Understanding Christian Images.* Brewster, MA: Paraclete, 2012.
Daily, Eileen M. *Beyond the Written Word: Exploring Faith Through Christian Art.* Winona, MN: St. Mary's, 2005.
Dawtry, Anne, and Christian Irvine. *Art and Worship.* Collegeville, MN: Liturgical, 2002.
De Beaufort, Joseph. *Brother Lawrence: the practice of the presence of God the best rule of a holy life, being conversations and letters of Nicholas Herman of Lorraine (Brother Lawrence).* Translated from the French. New York: Fleming H. Revell, 2022.
De Borchgrave, Helen. *Journey into Christian Art.* Minneapolis: Augsburg Fortress, 2000.
Derrick, John C. "Painted Church." https://www.hawaii-guide.com/big-island/sights/painted_church.
Dillenberger, Jane. *Style and Content in Christian Art.* Eugene, OR: Wipf & Stock, 2005.
Drevitch, Gary. "Why a Love of the Arts Will Help Your Brain Age Better." Nextavenue, Sep 12, 2012. https://www.nextavenue.org/why-love-arts-will-help-your-brain-age-better/
Dyrness, William. *Senses of the Soul: Art and the Visual in Christian Worship.* Eugene, OR: Cascade, 2008.
———. *Visual Faith: Art, Theology, and Worship in Dialogue.* Grand Rapids: Baker Academic, 2001.
Eatman, George, and James Simpson. *A Treasury of Anglican Art.* New York: Rizzoli, 2003.
Ferguson, George. *Signs and Symbols in Christian Art: With Illustrations from Paintings from the Renaissance.* New York: Oxford University Press, 1954.
Fichner-Rathus, Lois. *Understanding Art.* 10th ed. Boston: Wadsworth, 2013.
Fleming, Daniel Johnson. *Each with His Own Brush: Contemporary Christian Art in Asia and Africa.* New York: Friendship, 1938.
Finaldi, Gabriele. *The Image of Christ.* London: National Gallery, 2011.
Finney, Paul Corby. *The Invisible God: The Earliest Christians on Art.* New York: Oxford University Press, 1994.
Fliegel, Stephen, ed. *A Higher Contemplation: Sacred Meaning in the Christian Art of the Middle Ages.* Kent, OH: Kent State University Press, 2012.
Forest, Jim. *Praying with Icons.* Revised, expanded ed. Maryknoll, NY: Orbis, 2008.
Gaebelein, Frank E. *The Christian, the Arts and Truth: Regaining the Vision of Greatness.* Portland, OR: Multnomah Press, 1985.

Gallaty, Robby. *Rediscovering Discipleship: Making Jesus' Final Words Our First Work.* Grand Rapids: Zondervan, 2015.

Gerding, Jeri. *Drawing to God: Art as Prayer, Prayer as Art.* Notre Dame, IN: Sorin, 2001.

Giorgi, Rosa. *The Saints: A Year in Faith and Art.* New York: Abrams, 2006.

———. *Saints and Their Symbols.* New York: Abrams, 2012.

Goodman, Stacey. "7 Ways Art Supports Interdisciplinary Work." Edutopia, Dec 13, 2016. https://www.edutopia.org/blog/7-ways-art-supports-interdisciplinary-work-stacey-goodman.

Gorringe, Timothy J. *Earthly Visions: Theology and the Challenges of Art.* New Haven: Yale University Press, 2011.

Gough, Michael. *The Origins of Christian Art.* Santa Barbara, CA: Praeger, 1974.

Gustafson, Dwight. *A Brighter Witness: Conversations on the Christian and the Arts.* Greenville, SC: BJU, 2012.

———. *The History of the Church in Art (A Guide to Imagery).* Los Angeles: John Paul Getty Museum, 2009.

Hamburger, Jeffrey, and Anne-Marie Bouché, eds. *The Mind's Eye: Art and Theological Argument in the Middle Ages.* Princeton, NJ: Princeton University Press, 2005.

Harries, Richard. *The Image of Christ in Modern Art.* Burlington, VT: Ashgate, 2013.

Harris, Marta, "Introduction" to *Imaging the Word: An Arts and Lectionary Resource*, vol. 3, 9-13. Susan A. Blain, ed. Cleveland: United Church Press, 1996.

Hart, Thomas N. *The Art of Christian Listening.* Mahwah, NJ: Paulist, 1980.

Hart, Trevor, Gavin Hopps, and Jeremy Begbie, eds. *Art, Imagination and Christian Hope: Patterns of Promise.* Burlington, VT: Ashgate, 2012.

Holtam, Nicholas. *The Art of Worship: Paintings, Prayers, and Readings for Meditation.* London, UK: National Gallery London, 2011.

Hourihane, Colum. *Image and Belief.* Princeton, NJ: Princeton University Press, 1999.

Jackson, Candace. "How Art Affects the Brain: A New Exhibit Explores Science and Aesthetics." *Wall Street Journal*, Jan 22, 2010. https://www.wsj.com/articles/SB10001424052748703699204575017050699693576.

Jensen, Eric. *Arts with the Brain in Mind.* Alexandria, VA: Association for Supervision and Curriculum Development, 2001.

Jensen, Robin Margaret. *Understanding Early Christian Art.* New York: Routledge, 2000.

Kalnin, Jim, and Lois Huey-Heck. *The Spirituality of Art.* Kelowna, British Columbia: Wood Lake, 2006.

Kandinsky, Wassily. *Concerning the Spiritual in Art.* Translated by M. T. H. Sadler. New York: Dover, 1977.

Kapakian, Catherine. *Art in the Service of the Sacred.* Edited by Kathy Black. Nashville: Abingdon, 2006.

Keller, David G. R. *Oasis of Wisdom: The Worlds of the Desert Fathers and Mothers.* Collegeville, MN: Liturgical Press, 2005.

Kretzmann, Paul E. *Christian Art: In the Place and in the Form of Lutheran Worship.* St. Louis: Concordia, 1921.

Kuchan, Karen. *Visio Divina: A New Practice of Prayer for Healing and Growth.* New York: Crossroad, 2005.

Lang, J. Stephen. *Christian History Devotional: 365 Readings & Prayers to Deepen and Inspire Your Faith.* Nashville: Thomas Nelson, 2012.

Lehmann, Arno. *Christian Art in Africa and Asia.* St. Louis: Concordia, 1969.

L'Engle, Madeleine. *Walking on Water: Reflections on Faith and Art*. Wheaton, IL: Harold Shaw, 1980.

Loverance, Rowena. *Christian Art*. Cambridge, MA: Harvard University Press, 2007.

MacBeth, Sybil. *Praying in Color: Drawing a New Path to God*. Expanded edition. Brewster, MA: Paraclete Press, 2019.

Martin, Linette. *Sacred Doorways: A Beginner's Guide to Icons*. Brewster, MA: Paraclete Press, 2006.

McCullough, James. *Sense and Spirituality: The Arts and Spiritual Formation*. Eugene, OR: Cascade, 2015.

Merton, Thomas. *New Seeds of Contemplation*. Reprint ed. New York: New Directions, 2007.

Mixa, Robert. "Beauty and Religious Life." Vocation Blog, Sep 29, 2017. https://vocationblog.com/2017/09/beauty-and-religious-life.

Moon, Gary W. and David G. Benner. eds. *Spiritual Direction and the Care of Souls: A Guide to Christian Approaches and Practices*. Downers Grove: InterVarsity Press, 2004.

Morneau, Robert F. *Spiritual Direction: A Path to Spiritual Maturity*. New York: Crossroad, 1992.

Murray, Peter, and Linda Murray. *The Oxford Companion to Christian Art and Architecture*. New York: Oxford University Press, 1996.

———. *The Dictionary of Christian Art & Architecture*, 2nd ed. Edited by Tom Devonshire Jones. Oxford, UK: Oxford University Press, 2013.

Nemeck, Francis Kelly and Marie Theresa Coombs. *The Way of Spiritual Direction*. Collegeville, MN: Liturgical Press, 1985.

Nes, Solrunn. *The Mystical Language of Icons*. Grand Rapids: Eerdmans, 2004.

Nouwen, Henri, Michael J. Christensen, and Rebecca J. Laird. *Spiritual Direction: Wisdom for the Long Walk of Faith*. New York: HarperOne, 2006.

O'Donahue, John. *Anam Cara: A Book of Celtic Wisdom*, 25th ed. New York: Harper Perennial, 2022.

Paintner, Christine Valters. *Eyes of the Heart: Photography as a Christian Contemplative Practice*. Notre Dame, IN: Sorin, 2013.

Pelikan, Jaroslav. *The Illustrated Jesus Through the Centuries*. New Haven: Yale University Press, 1997.

Peters, Thomas C. *The Christian Imagination: G. K. Chesterton and the Arts*. San Francisco: Ignatius, 2000.

Pieper, Josef. *Only the Lover Sings: Art and Contemplation*. San Francisco: Ignatius, 1990.

Quenot, Michel. *The Resurrection and the Icon*. Yonkers, NY: St. Vladimir's Seminary, 1998.

Ramshaw, Gail. *Christian Worship: 100,000 Sundays of Symbols and Rituals*. Minneapolis: Fortress, 2009.

Rest, Fredrich. *Our Christian Symbols*. Cleveland: Pilgrim, 1954.

Rice, D. Talbot. *The Beginnings of Christian Art*. Nashville: Abingdon, 1957.

Robinson, Jennifer. *Deeper Than Reason: Emotion and its Role in Literature, Music, and Art*. New York: Oxford University Press, 2005.

Ross, Maggie. *Silence: A User's Guide*. Vol. 1. Eugene, OR: Cascade, 2014.

———. *Writing the Icon of the Heart*. Eugene, OR: Cascade, 2013.

Ryken, Philip Graham. *Art for God's Sake: A Call to Recover the Arts*. Philipsburg, NJ: P & R, 2006.

Scorgie, Glen G. *A Little Guide to Christian Spirituality: Three Dimensions of Life with God.* Grand Rapids: Zondervan, 2007.

Schaeffer, Francis A. and Michael Card. *Art and the Bible.* Downers Grove: InterVarsity, 2006.

Shanley, Brother Aelred-Seton, ed., Thierry Bondroit, Odette Mukherjee, and Joseph Schlipf, illustrators. *Clip Art of the Christian World: Christian Art from its Origins to the Fifteenth Century.* New York: Pueblo, 1990.

Shea, John. *Stories of God: An Unauthorized Biography.* Chicago: Thomas More Press, 1978.

Siedell, Jeffrey, Robert Johnston, and William Dyrness. *God in the Gallery: A Christian Embrace of Modern Art.* Grand Rapids: Baker Academic, 2008.

Sink, Susan. *The Art of the Saint John's Bible: The Complete Reader's Guide.* Collegeville: Liturgical, 2013.

Smith, Gordon T. *Spiritual Direction: A Guide to Giving and Receiving Spiritual Direction.* Downers Grove: InterVarsity, 2014.

Sokolove, Deborah. *Sanctifying Art: Inviting Conversation Between Artists, Theologians, and the Church.* Eugene, OR: Cascade, 2003.

Soneff, Sharon and Mindy Caliguire. *Faith Books & Spiritual Journaling: Expressions of Faith Through Art.* Gloucester, MA: Quarry, 2006.

Spier, Jeffrey, Herbert L. Kessler, Steven Fine, and Mary Charles-Murray. *Picturing the Bible: the Earliest Christian Art.* New Haven: Yale University Press, 2009.

Stasi, Lauri. *Shadow Painter: A Practical Handbook for Prophetic Christian Art.* Macon, GA: Good News Fellowship Ministries, 2013

"St. Brigid of Ireland." 2020. https://thedailymass.com/st-brigid-of-ireland.

The Saint John's Bible. https://stjohnsbible.org.

Stemp, Richard. *The Secret Language of Churches and Cathedrals: Decoding the Sacred Symbolism of Christianity's Holy Buildings.* London: Duncan Baird, 2010.

Sullivan, Jem. *The Beauty of Faith: Using Christian Art to Spread the Good News.* Huntington, IN: Our Sunday Visitor, 2009.

Sullivan, Michael Radford. *Windows Into the Soul: Art as Spiritual Experience.* Harrisburg, PA: Morehouse, 2006.

Swanson, John August. "Praying With Art—Visio Divina." https://www.patheos.com/resources/additional-resources/2009/07/praying-with-art-visio-divina.

Taylor, Richard. *How to Read a Church: A Gide to Symbols and Images in Churches and Cathedrals.* Mahwah, NJ: HiddenSpring, 2005.

Toman, Rolf, ed. *ARS SACRA: Christian Art in the Western World.* Potsdam, Germany: Ullman, 2010.

Treier, Daniel J., Mark Husbands, and Roger Lundin. *The Beauty of God: Theology and the Arts.* Downers Grove: Intervarsity, 2007.

Trotter, F. Thomas "What Is Religious Art?" https://www.religion-online.org/article/what-is-religious-art.

Turner, Steve. *A Vision of Christians in the Arts.* Downers Grove: InterVarsity, 2001.

uCatholic. "St. Brigid of Ireland." No pages. Online: https://ucatholic.com/saints/brigid of-ireland/.

Viladesau, Richard. *Theology and the Arts: Encountering God Through Music, Art and Rhetoric.* Mahwah, NJ: Paulist Press, 2000.

Visel, Jeana. *Icons in the Western Church: Toward a More Sacramental Encounter.* Collegeville, MN: Liturgical Press, 2016.

von Hildebrand, Dietrich. *Aesthetics*. Vol. 1. Translated by Brian McNeil. Steubenville, OH: The Hildebrand Legacy Project, 2016.

———. *Transformation in Christ: On the Christian Attitude*. San Francisco: Ignatius, 1976.

von Hildebrand, Dietrich, and Robert E. Wood. *Aesthetics*, Volume 1. Steubenville, OH: Hildebrand Legacy Project, 2016.

Wilder, Amos N. "The Church's New Concern with the Arts." *Christianity and Crisis XVII* (Feb 1957) 12–14.

Williamson, Beth. *Christian Art: A Very Short Introduction*. New York: Oxford University Press, 2004.

Wolterstorff, Nicholas. *Art in Action: Towards a Christian Aesthetic*. Grand Rapids: Eerdmans, 1987.

Wooddell, Joseph L. *The Beauty of the Faith: Using Aesthetics for Christian Apolog*etics. Eugene, OR: Wipf & Stock, 2011.

Wight, Susan. *The Bible in Art*. New York: Smithmark, 1996.

Yoon, Jungu. *Spirituality in Contemporary Art*. London: Zidane, 2010.

Zaczek, Ian, and Mary Acton. *Art: Over 2,500 Works from Cave to Contemporary*. London: Dorling Kindersley, 2008.

Zambon, Kat. "How Engaging With Art Affects the Human Brain." AAAS, Nov 13, 2013. https://www.aaas.org/news/how-engaging-art-affects-human-brain.

www.ingramcontent.com/pod-product-compliance
Lightning Source LLC
LaVergne TN
LVHW010037160826
845671LV00003B/163

* 9 7 8 1 4 9 8 2 8 5 4 2 1 *